ELIZABETH J MUSHENO

SEWING SHORTCUTS FROM A TO Z

CROSBY LOCKWOOD STAPLES
GRANADA PUBLISHING
London Toronto Sydney New York

Published by Granada Publishing Limited
in Crosby Lockwood Staples 1979

Granada Publishing Limited
Frogmore, St Albans, Herts AL2 2NF
and
3 Upper James Street, London W1R 4BP
1221 Avenue of the Americas, New York, NY 10020 USA
117 York Street, Sydney, NSW 2000, Australia
100 Skyway Avenue, Toronto, Ontario, Canada M9W 3A6
110 Northpark Centre, 2193 Johannesburg, South Africa
CML Centre, Queen & Wyndham Auckland 1,
New Zealand

Copyright © 1978 by Litton Educational Publishing, Inc.

ISBN 0 258 97124 X

Printed in Great Britain by
Fletcher & Son Ltd, Norwich

CONTENTS

Acknowledgments

The many years spent making clothes for my five daughters, Sharon, Adelade, Yvonne, Cathy, and Deborah impelled me to develop many sewing shortcuts. They even volunteered my services to make costumes for every school play and operetta and majorette uniforms when the school band could not afford to buy them. It wasn't long before I was sewing dancing costumes for the local dance recitals, too.

When I worked as a sewing room teacher for The Singer Company, women often brought their mistakes in and asked me how they could salvage a garment. And finally I acquired technical knowledge while working for the Butterick Fashion Marketing Company and helping them to produce Vogue and Butterick patterns, all the Vogue sewing books, and the Butterick sewing book, *Ready! Set! Sew!*

Throughout this book expert photographs by Scott Hyde and technical drawings by Marie Martin illustrate and enhance the text.

The fabric and notions people were most helpful, especially Herman Phynes of Fabrications, Jennifer Butler of Spring Mills, Pat McCarthey of Burlington, and Anna Bozzi of David Traum Inc.

There is hardly a book published for which the author does not receive moral support, such as I did, from my agent, Ray Pierre Corsini and my editor, Nancy Newman Green.

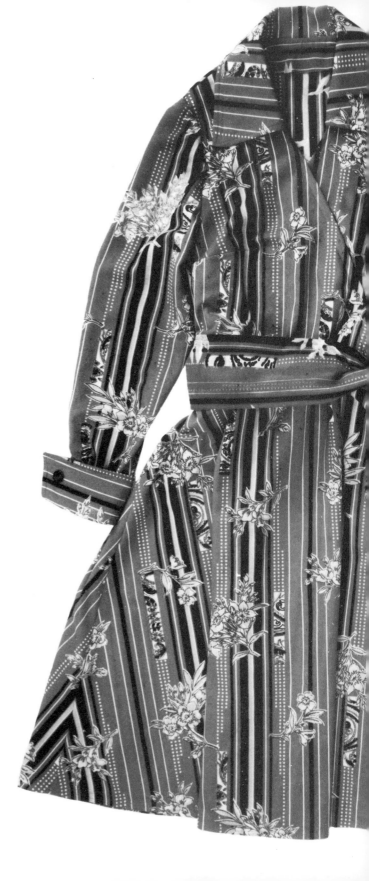

A NEW APPROACH TO SEWING

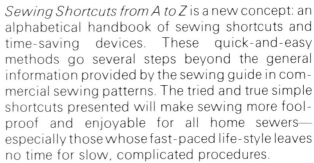

Sewing Shortcuts from A to Z is a new concept: an alphabetical handbook of sewing shortcuts and time-saving devices. These quick-and-easy methods go several steps beyond the general information provided by the sewing guide in commercial sewing patterns. The tried and true simple shortcuts presented will make sewing more fool-proof and enjoyable for all home sewers—especially those whose fast-paced life-style leaves no time for slow, complicated procedures.

This book includes construction techniques that will appeal to the innovative, creative home sewer who can substitute machine stitching for many of the classic hand-sewn procedures. Even the fashion-conscious can use these carefree sewing methods for their "designer" patterns made with the wash-and-wear fabrics so popular today.

Those who enjoy sewing clothes for themselves and their family will find the step-by-step illustrated shortcuts easy to follow. As you turn the pages of this book, you will find ways to sew up a wardrobe in record time and still have garments that are well-made and fashionable.

Make your next 'designer' pattern entirely by machine. This dress was made from a stable knit that is easy to sew and does not require any raw-edge finishes. Even the hem is stitched in place with two rows of top-stitching on the front, neck, and collar edges.

HOW TO USE THIS BOOK

First read the next section, A Fast Start, and then browse through the alphabetical section. You will find many techniques and sewing shortcuts that will save you time every time you sew. Then use the book often as a handy reference.

Hundreds of line drawings illustrate each step. In order to make the sketches easier to understand, shading is used to indicate the right side of the fabric, the wrong side of the fabric, interfacing, underlining, the right side of the lining, and the wrong side of the lining.

Some photographs of garment construction show stitching with contrasting coloured thread so that it will be seen easily. When using these procedures, be sure to use thread that matches your fabric so it will be nearly invisible.

Explanatory notes appear through the alphabetical entries to give special information. If included in the step-by-step procedures, these tips might make them long or confusing. These tips are being preceded by the word "Note."

Cross-references that are used throughout the alphabetical section are italicized, eliminating the need for an index.

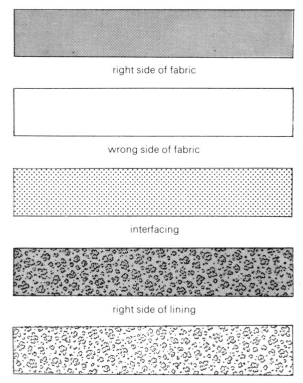

right side of fabric

wrong side of fabric

interfacing

right side of lining

wrong side of lining

A FAST START

To speed up sewing, some basic steps must be re-thought. Think about the amount of time that can be allotted to each project so it can be utilized effectively. Be realistic about your capabilities . . . don't underestimate how long it will take to cut, mark, and sew. If you are working against a dead-line, allow for interruptions—the phone, a child's feeding, a neighbour dropping in. They can upset the best plans.

Think about your life-style. How much uninter-rupted time can you devote to sewing? Will you be able to start and finish a sewing project on the same day, or must you sew piecemeal? Some of the busiest sewers break up the basic steps to fit them into their hectic schedule.

Think about patterns and fabric. An easy-to-make pattern may become complicated if you choose a fabric that requires special handling from beginning to end. Other patterns with fashion details may be completed quickly and easily with fabric that allows you to use the many sewing shortcuts in the alphabetical section.

Think about construction. Are you comfortable with the classic procedures? Are you looking for some quick and easy shortcuts? As you explore the shortcuts that are possible you may decide to incorporate some of each. Its quite possible that you may switch construction techniques to match your mood—hand-sew a few steps to relax frazzled nerves or sew up a storm with the many machine-sewn-finishes when you're pressed for time.

And finally, think out each basic step and how to get as much sewing done in the shortest possible time. There are four steps—planning, pattern selection, fabric selection and organization—that must be followed.

Step 1. Planning

This first step is most important—careful planning saves considerable time and energy. If you can't afford a lot of time for sewing but you want to make some additions to your own or another family member's wardrobe, you must decide what is needed most.

Make garments and accessories that will com-pliment those pieces that can be used for another season. You can make a weekend or vacation wardrobe using a single colour scheme, or one that will mix or match all the pieces. This kind of plan-ning seems to enlarge a basically small wardrobe and simplifies your packing problem. Even when adding just one garment or outfit to a wardrobe don't make an impulsive purchase and then find out that new shoes, bag, or other accessories may be needed before it can be worn.

A classic shirt with a front band and a one-piece collar and neck-band is an excellent style to adapt for a jacket. This one was made entirely by machine.

Step 2. Pattern Selection vs Time

The major pattern companies have done some spade work for you. They all offer easy-to-sew designs that have a limited number of pattern pieces with a minimum of details requiring less sewing time. Today's fashions are adapted for quick and easy sewing shortcuts. For example, the layered look often includes an unlined cape or coat for the top layer, a jacket and/or vest for the next layer worn with a blouse or top; then finished off with a skirt, pants, or gauchos as the innermost layer.

Just remember, the more seams and design features, the more time it will take to sew. However, if a detailed pattern is more to your liking, simply incorporate all the sewing shortcuts presented here and your garment will go together quicker than ever.

You do not have to be limited by the patterns available for any one garment. When you find an attractive pattern that fits well, adapt it to make other things. Throughout the alphabetical section you will find methods such as casings, pleats, sleeves, etc., that tell you how to alter a pattern to make these changes.

Suppose you have a pattern for a blouse or shirt, or a button-front or wrap-dress and you would like to use it to make an unlined jacket, coat, or robe. It is quite simple to enlarge the pattern so the garment can be worn over another one just like it. Remember, each layer of fabric that drapes over the body must hang free and clear and not be too tight or the underneath layer will buckle, causing wrinkles and ridges on the outer layer.

This wool suit was made by using a classic shirt pattern and a gored skirt pattern. The jacket was lined, using the *lining* method 2. Shaped vents were made at the ends of the side seams and a narrow tie belt was added. The results are a smartly tailored suit made entirely by machine with hammer-on snap fasteners.

Simply add 13 mm to each side (A) and sleeve (B) seam edge. For medium- to heavy-weight fabrics, add 13 mm to the cuff too, if used. When a collar buttons snugly around the neck add 13 mm to the centre back of both the collar and the garment if you want to close it over a turtleneck sweater.

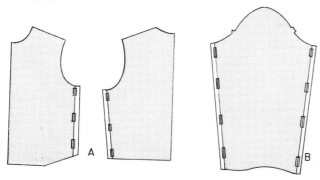

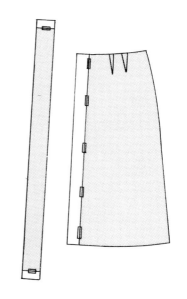

An A-line skirt has always been a favourite basic silhouette and it can be adapted to suit the changing styles. To add pleats, see the alphabetical section. To make a buttoned front, add 94 mm to centre fold: 25 mm for the lap so buttons or other fasteners may be used and 70 mm for a facing. Cut two front pieces. Match centre backs of the waistband; pin. Split waistband pattern at centre front and add 40 mm to each end: 25 mm for the lap and 15 mm for a seam allowance. Cut as many waistband sections as needed.

To change a neckline of a favourite well-fitting garment, cut out the front pattern on the fold from newspaper or any other type of paper available. Draw in the proposed new neckline and cut out. Hold pattern over the body to see where the neckline falls. When the shape and location is satisfactory, add a 15 mm seam allowance (A). To make a facing, use the new neckline with the 15 mm seam allowance added on and the shoulder edge. Cut out this shape and then make a 70 mm deep facing by measuring from the new cutting lines between the shoulder and centre front edges, moving the ruler about 25 mm at a time. Shape the marks into a smooth line (B). Note: There are many finishes such as bias binding and bias facings that may be substituted for a facing.

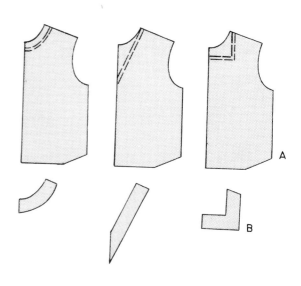

Step 3. Fast and Foolproof Fabrics

Your fabric choice will be a deciding factor, too. Select fabric that is easy to cut and sew and that does not ravel, so the seam allowances do not need to be *clean-finished*. When making pattern adaptations as suggested in some of the short-cut procedures or in Step 2, be sure to purchase additional fabric, if necessary.

Fabrics that are tightly woven or knitted are the best choice. Prints, stripes, and plaids that require matching will require more cutting and sewing time, but there are ways to speed up these procedures.

Knits are popular because of their wash-and-wear properties. Be sure to choose the type recommended by your pattern. Stable knits may be used for any type of garment pattern while stretchable knits should be used with patterns specifically designed for them.

Favourite **woven fabrics** that are easy to sew are gabardine, denim, chino, linen, homespun, calico, chintz, percale, broadcloth, Indian muslin, wool flannel, and many of the new synthetics and blends that have the same characteristics as these fabrics.

Some fabrics, such as denim, require seam allowances to be finished to prevent fraying. Machine zigzag or overcast them or use a *flat-felled seam* or a *French seam substitute*.

Bonded fabrics are still available. Cut as it comes from the bolt since the ends cannot be straightened.

There are some lovely **Sheers** and **open-work** fabrics that are easy to sew, too. Sheers are especially useful for unstructured garments which eliminate *interfacings*. Trim enclosed seam allowances to 3 mm with pinking shears so the edges will be attractive.

Light- and medium-weight **corduroy** and **velveteen** are quite easy to handle. It only takes a little more time to cut them out. If the pattern does not give a "with nap" cutting layout, additional fabric may be required. Be sure to check the cutting guide to see how many pieces are placed against the nap. Make a test seam and adjust the machine's presser foot pressure, if necessary.

Fake fur, **leather**, and suede require a few special sewing techniques. Use a pattern with as few seams as possible, with minimum easing and darts. Remove excess ease from set-in sleeve caps, if required. Be sure to make a test seam and adjust pressure of machine's presser foot. For fake fur be careful not to cut the hairs. Cut one layer at a time using only the tip of the shears or a razor blade. On the right side of a seam, use a darning needle to pull the hairs free from the stitching. Follow manufacturer's instructions for pressing.

This sheer voile blouse was cut out with pinking shears to eliminate the need for seam finishes. All interfacing was omitted. The enclosed seams were trimmed with pinking shears too, making it a handsome unstructured blouse.

When cutting out fake leathers or suede, pin pattern pieces in place in the seam allowances to prevent puncture marks on the garment, or use weights. For some types save fabric by eliminating one seam allowance, then finishing with a lapped and top-stitched seam. To make, lap the trimmed garment section 15 mm over the untrimmed seam allowance. Stitch 3 mm from trimmed edge and stitch again 6 mm away.

To insert a zipper, trim away 13 mm from the extended seam allowance. Place zipper underneath and stitch in place. On the trimmed layer, stitch 3 mm from cut edge the length of the zipper.

Then, lap this garment edge over the untrimmed seam allowance 15 mm. Stitch 3 mm from cut edge connecting with previous stitches and again 6 mm away continuing across remaining zipper tape.

When making collar and lapels, shape them the same as the instructions for a *collar, method* 5. Trim away the outer edges along the under-collar and the front opening seamlines. Stitch 3 mm from cut edges and again 6 mm away.

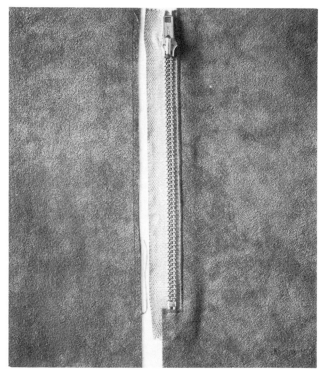

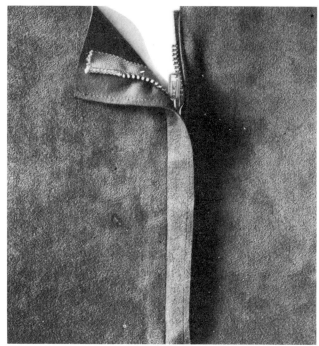

Step 4. Organization

Time is a most important factor to all who sew, and those who are well organized can complete a garment faster and easier.

Study your pattern's cutting and sewing guide. It was planned with great care and will start you off on the right foot. The sewing instructions were developed to show the garment being stitched together piece by piece and construction methods will work for all fabrics suggested on the pattern envelope. However, there are shortcuts that will speed up the whole process and still result in a fashionable, well-made garment.

If you plan to work straight through, set up the ironing board near the sewing machine and lay out all pressing equipment. Gather all cutting, measuring, and marking equipment and put it with the fabric and pattern. Place all sewing implements near the sewing machine. You are now ready to begin!

If you are working for short periods of time, divide your work plan in the same way, gathering and setting up the equipment needed for each phase. It's quite possible to make a garment in your spare time without ever feeling pressured. Break down the major steps according to the time available. If you do not have a sewing corner or room, plan to set up the sewing machine and ironing board in an out-of-the-way spot so it's available whenever you can spare a little time.

Cutting and *marking:* You will need scissors, pins, tape measure and other measuring equipment, tracing wheel and dressmaker's carbon or other marking tools, and a large flat surface.

Make needed pattern adjustments and/or alterations.

Cut out everything needed for the whole sewing project: *fashion fabric, interfacing,* and *lining.*

Cut out tightly woven fabrics with pinking shears to save time—the seam allowances won't need any other finish. Cut carefully along the outside of the cutting line making sure the inner edge of the teeth does not go inside the pattern's cutting line.

To mark fabric quickly see the *marking* methods in the alphabetical section.

For the busy person this step can be done in several phases: Make pattern adjustments and/or alterations; cut fashion fabric; cut out interfacing and lining; mark fabric and pin all darts and uncrossed seams.

Stitching and *pressing:* Have your sewing machine and ironing board as close together as possible to save steps and time, and have all other equipment within easy reach.

Think about flat and assembly-line procedures as you plan. Flat construction is used by factories and each operator stitches just one phase of the construction to save time and speed up produc-

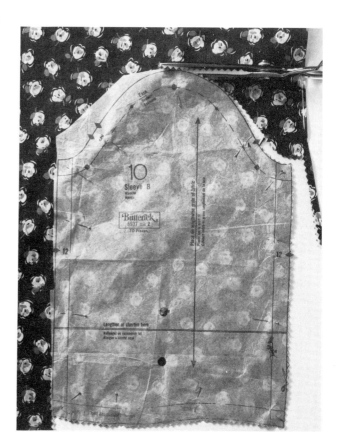

tion. You can do the same. Pin or fuse interfacing to all matching fabric sections; insert zipper in a seam while garment sections are flat; at one time stitch all darts and seams that do not cross another seam or dart; stitch, trim, and grade at the same time the enclosed seam edges of collars, cuffs, belts, etc.; then press; add *ease threads* and make openings in sleeve. By now you should have some shortcut ideas of your own to speed up sewing your garment together.

High-fashion designers frown upon flat construction. They feel that you do not get the same look when sleeves or pant legs are stitched together on the flat. However, with labour costs escalating many name-brand garments are stitched by the flat method. When the completed sleeves are stitched in the armhole or the pant legs are joined in a continuous crotch seam, the sleeves hang close to the garment and the pant legs hang side by side. When they are stitched by the flat method, some fabric may be rigid enough to cause the sleeve to hang out away from the garment at the underarm and the pant legs may separate giving a keyhole look that is rounded where the seams are crossed; the legs separate above the knees, and the sleeves hang away from the garment above the elbow. Men's shirts and the ever popular blue jeans have always been sewn on the flat and they are comfortable—so don't be afraid to try flat construction.

Naturally, there's a choice: If you try inserting classic sleeves on the flat and don't like it, revert to the set-in method for sleeves. Finish the front and back openings and neck edges before the side seams are stitched and the garment is relatively flat—this is still the quickest and easiest way for these fashion details. When the side seams are stitched, insert the completed sleeve.

To *stitch* a blouse, jacket, or shirt together, use this procedure: Stitch darts in front and back sections and stitch the shoulder seams (A). Now press darts and seams. Make collar and cuffs (B).

Clean-finish facing edges and stitch together (C). Baste collar in place and then stitch on facing (D).

Stitch sleeves in armhole; stitch side and under-

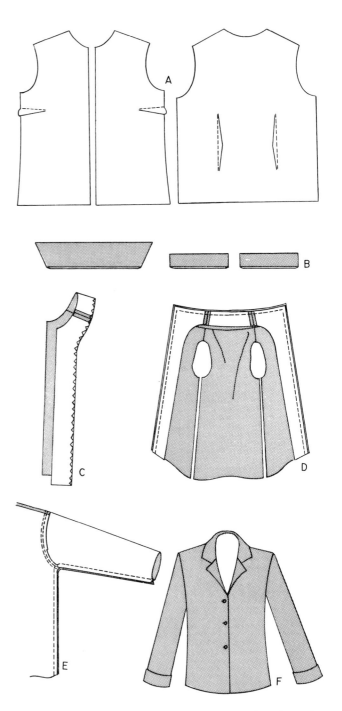

arm seams (E); stitch cuff to sleeves; stitch hem in place; and sew on buttons or attach snap fasteners (F).

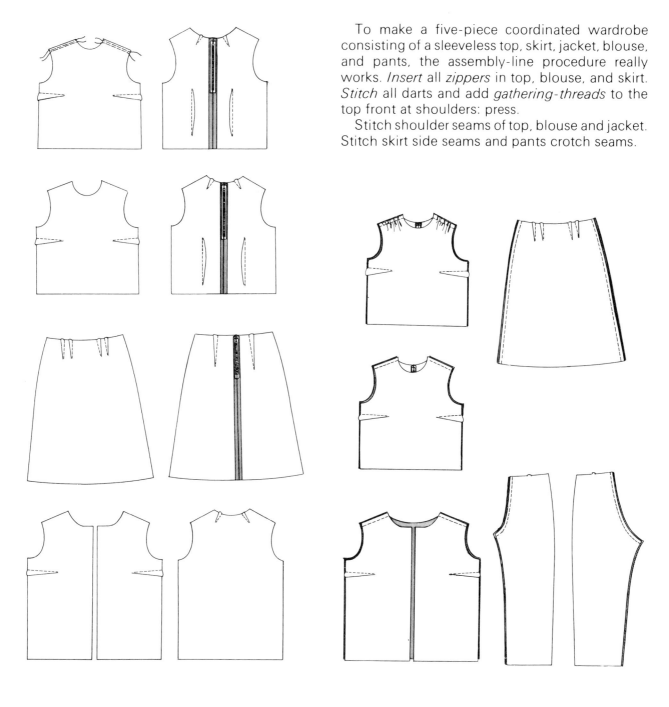

To make a five-piece coordinated wardrobe consisting of a sleeveless top, skirt, jacket, blouse, and pants, the assembly-line procedure really works. *Insert* all *zippers* in top, blouse, and skirt. *Stitch* all darts and add *gathering-threads* to the top front at shoulders: press.

Stitch shoulder seams of top, blouse and jacket. Stitch skirt side seams and pants crotch seams.

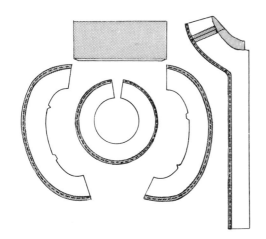

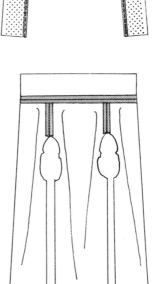

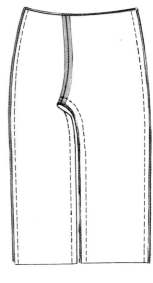

Make *collar* for blouse. Stitch top neck facings together; stitch jacket facings together and *clean-finish* all the facings edges.

Position *interfacing;* stitch undercollar to jacket and stitch the upper collar to the facing. Stitch side and inseams of pants.

Stitch neck and armhole facings to top; attach collar to blouse; stitch upper collar and facings to undercollar and jacket. *Trim, clip, notch, grade,* and *press* as needed.

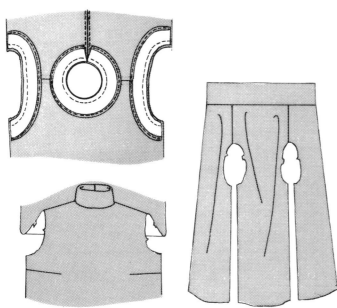

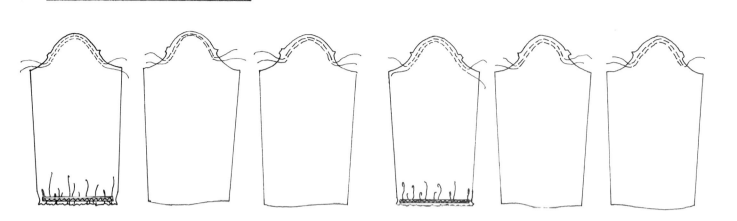

Make waistband for skirt; apply elastic to blouse sleeve edges and add *ease-threads* to blouse and jacket sleeves.

Stitch side seams of top and armhole facings; stitch sleeves to armhole of blouse and jacket.

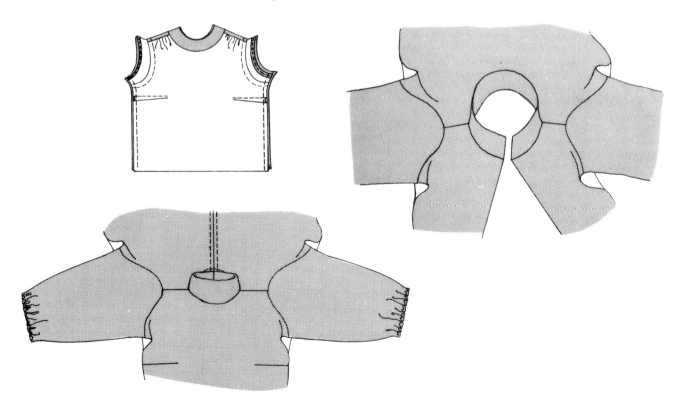

Stitch blouse and jacket side and sleeve seams. Attach waistband to skirt and make elasticized *casing* in pants. Make all hems in top, blouse, skirt, pants and jacket.

Simply vary these procedures to accommodate the type of garments you have selected.

Sewing for men, boys, and toddlers is no longer any different from sewing for women and girls. Men, large or small, young or old, are now wearing as many knits as women, and everyone wears denim garments. These easy-care clothes are made as simply as possible with a few tailored details.

Handsome blazers and leisure jackets can be made by using the many quick and easy shortcuts found in the alphabetical section. Remember, men's and boys' patterns are now designed for the home-sewer and all the classic styles as well as sportswear are shown in every major pattern company's catalogue.

Classic shirts are made the same for both men and women and boys and girls, only the opening buttons are reversed. Many of the time-saving wash-and-wear fabrics cannot be *top-stitched* satisfactorily because the fabric puckers, so *flat-felled* seams have been eliminated by clothing manufacturers and you should do the same.

Stitch the *structural seams*, but do not press them open and finish the edges in one of two ways: Trim the seam allowances to 6 mm and zigzag (A), or use the overcast stitch (B). Or make an easy French seam substitute by turning in the raw edges to meet the seam and then stitching them together (C).

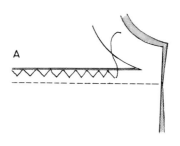

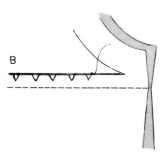

Sewing for toddlers and young children presents a problem because everything is so small. Flat construction is usually the quickest and easiest way to make a garment for these little people. Avoid garments with cuffs for the smallest sizes, if possible. Naturally it doesn't take long to sew two tiny band cuffs in place after they have been joined to the sleeves on the flat.

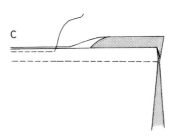

Sewing Shortcuts from A to Z is a blessing in disguise for the busy mother—using easy-care fabrics and these shortcuts, she can finish the entire garment by machine. For sportswear and play clothes, use the longest machine stitch to secure the hems in place. Then as the child grows taller, it's quite easy to let down the hem. When there is no more fabric to let out, add a contrasting band of fabric or trim for the extra length needed. If you choose to set-in the band, remember you will lose some length when the two seams needed to insert the band are stitched.

Sewing has always been a favourite craft of many and this book is intended to lighten the load for the busy craftswoman who wants to fit more sewing into her life-style.

SEWING SHORTCUT METHODS

A

Adjustments
The changes to be made on a commercial pattern's length and/or girth to adjust it to your measurements when they differ from the standard body measurements listed for the size you selected. Be sure to make any needed adjustments before cutting out your garment so you will get a better fit.

Alterations
1. Changes required on commercial patterns to accommodate individual figure difference (broad shoulders, wide hips, sway back, etc.) so that ample fabric will be available, or excess fabric will be eliminated before cutting out your garment to achieve a custom fit. 2. Changes that need to be made on a ready-to-wear garment to achieve a custom fit.

Anchor
To fasten something in place by *tacking, pinning, basting, stitching*, etc.

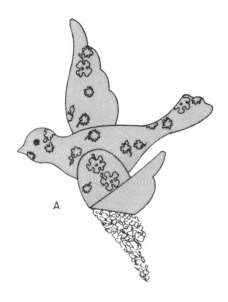

A

B

Appliqué

Technique for applying decorative patches on another material. There are many beautiful appliqués available, but creating your own can be most satisfying. There are several ways to fasten an appliqué to a garment or accessory that are quick and easy shortcuts.

1. Fusing: Cut desired shapes and use a *fusible* bonding agent to attach. When using a sheet of fusible material, cut same shape as appliqué. Fuse appliqué in place according to manufacturer's directions (A). These appliqués may also be zigzagged or hand-embroidered around their edges for a decorative effect.

2. Iron-on mending patches: Cut desired shapes, and affix to fabric following package instructions (B).

3. Machine: Cut out desired shapes. Machine baste or pin in place. Zigzag edges. When several layers of appliqué fall in the same place, zigzag only the top layer to avoid lumps (C).

C

Apply (applied)

Denotes a procedure where trims, ruffles, and fashion details are stitched to the outside of a garment as a decorative feature. Zippers may be applied to opening edges, waistband may be applied to a skirt or pant waist edge, and a ruffle may be applied to an edge with the correct preparatory steps.

Armhole facing

A strip of fabric that is *stitched* to the armhole of a sleeveless garment for a finished, enclosed edge. There are three types of armhole facing that are quick and easy to make: commercial single-fold bias tape, self-fabric bias, and a shaped facing.

To work on-the-flat, stitch shoulder seams and finish neck and opening edges as required.

1. Commercial single-fold bias tape: Press open one fold, then shape the tape to fit the armhole edge by stretching the remaining folded edge and shrinking the raw edge (A).

Pin to garment, placing crease of tape 15 mm from cut edge. *Stitch* along crease. *Trim* excess fabric even with tape, *clipping* underarm curves (B). Stitch side seam, continuing across bias (C).

Press side seams open, turning tape to the inside of the garment along seam, *favouring* garment edge; press. Pin in place. *Edgestitch* folded edge in place and again along the armhole edge (D). For special fabrics and garments, sew folded edge in place with *slip-stitch* method 1 (E).

2. Self bias: Cut two bias strips 38 mm wide, the length of the armhole edge plus 50 mm. Turn in one long edge 6 mm; press. Shape strip to fit armhole edge same as step A, above. Pin to garment, with raw edges even. *Stitch* 15 mm from raw edges. *Trim* seam; *clip* underarm curve (F). Complete steps C and D, stitching side seam and bias in one operation. Press seam allowances open and turn bias folding to inside *favouring* garment edge. Attach facing using steps D or E for the commercial bias tape.

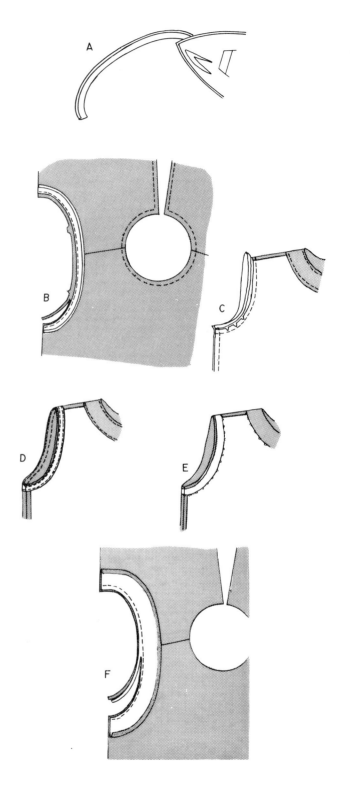

3. Shaped facing with clear-finished outer edge:
Stitch facing shoulder seams and *clean-finish*
outer unnotched edge. Pin facing to garment,
making raw edges even. *Stitch* armhole seam. *Trim*
and *clip* seam allowance. *Understitch*, keeping
facing flat as you stitch (A). Stitch side seams,
continuing across facing (B). Press seam open.

Turn facing to inside, *favouring* garment edge;
press. At shoulder and underarm seams, *tack* facing in place by machine (C), or by hand (D).

For combined neck and armhole facing, see
Neck and Armhole Combination.

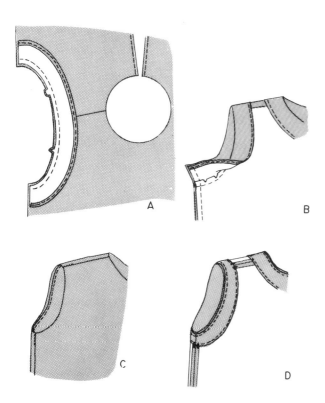

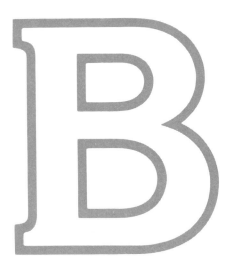

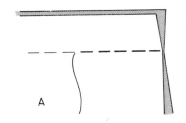

A

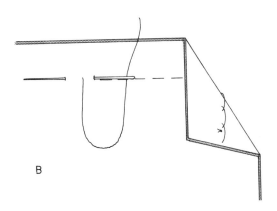

B

Backing

A layer of fabric that is placed under a layer of sheer, lace, or open-work fabric to make it opaque. Cut backing same as the decorative *fashion fabric*. Place wrong side of decorative fabric over right side of backing: pin. Machine-baste 13 mm from cut edges and through the centre of any darts same as for *underlining* and handle as one fabric layer throughout construction.

Back-stitch (back-tack)

1. A sewing-machine technique used to secure the thread ends of a row of stitches, eliminating the need to tie the threads so the seam ends will not pop open. Insert machine needle about 13 mm from seam end. Use machine lever to move the machine backwards to the edge of the fabric. When stitching forward, stitch carefully over the previous stitches so there is no lump when pressing a seam open (A).

2. A hand-stitch that is as strong as machine stitching. Use to mend or sew a zipper in place (B).

Make a large denim bag with three sizes of patch pockets. This bag is 30 cm wide, 45 cm long, and 10 cm deep with 55 cm long handles.

Bags (and handbags)

These are the easiest accessory to sew. Make them as large or as small as you like. All sorts of wooden and plastic handles can be purchased, and there are commercial patterns available for these types of handbags. However, if you want to make a simple bag or handbag that is washable here are two types. They can be plain or decorated with appliqués, pockets, or your favourite needlework. Use durable fabric such as ticking, denim, or any suitable medium- to heavy-weight fabric.

1. Bag: This can be as small as 20 cm × 25 cm and 10 cm deep with 30 cm handles or as large as you like, say, 30 cm × 45 cm and 10–15 cm deep with 55 cm long handles, large enough to carry over your shoulder. Make a pattern from newspaper. Draw a rectangle the size desired, add 10 cm for the bottom, and then another rectangle the same size. Add 5 cm to the top for hems and 6·5 cm to each long edge for the sides and seam allowances (A). Plan for the handles to be at least 2·5 cm wide when finished. Add 10 cm to the desired finished length, and cut the strip at least 8 cm wide for each handle including the seam allowance (B).

Stitch handle strips in a 15 mm seam, turn right side out and press. *Edge-stitch* seamed edge and again 6 mm away. Centre strips over each end of the bag, placing the handles at least 7·5 cm apart. Stitch ends to bag as shown, making the straight line 5 cm from the cut edge and reinforcing it with several rows of stitches. This is where the *hem* is turned in (C). Add patch *pockets* to the bag with the opening edges toward the handles about 10–15 cm from the raw ends.

If you want a more secure pocket add a zipper to the patch pocket.

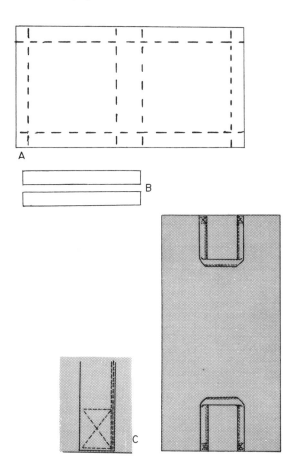

A small denim bag with a zippered pocket is a great size for lunches, shoes, and other small items you carry to work, school, or play. This bag is 20 cm wide, 25 cm long, and 10 cm deep with 30 cm long handles.

Cut a rectangle twice the desired finished width and as wide as desired. Turn in the ends 6 mm; *press*. *Lap* ends over the *zipper* tape and *edge-stitch* in place (A). Open the zipper, turn the wrong sides out, and fold above one zipper tape edge. *Stitch* each end in a 6 mm seam (B).

Turn right side out; press. Edge-stitch close to edge above the zipper and again 6 mm away (C). Edge-stitch side and lower edges to bag with opening toward handles; stitch again 6 mm away (D).

Fold bag in half, right sides together; stitch sides to within 25 mm of the fold. *Clean-finish* seam allowances, if necessary (E). Mark fold with pins. Place fold over seam, forming triangular ends; pin. Mark where the triangular ends measure 10 cm (5 cm on each side of the pin or seam). Draw a line across the ends at this point and stitch. Stitch again 6 mm away and trim corners (F). Turn in top edge and handles 5 cm to form hem; pin. Turn in raw edge 13 mm or clean-finish edge of heavy fabrics. Stitch hem in place and again 6 mm away (G).

To press bag, measure 5 cm from each seam; form a crease and press. Crease along end seam and press. Then crease across the bottom of the bag between the corners. Fold bag flat and press so it looks like a large, brown paper, grocery bag. This pressing forms the square shape of the bags in the photographs. If you want to make the creases permanent, edge-stitch close to each fold.

Note: This bag may be made with two sections instead of the one larger section. You will have a seam at the centre of the bottom too.

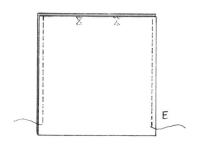

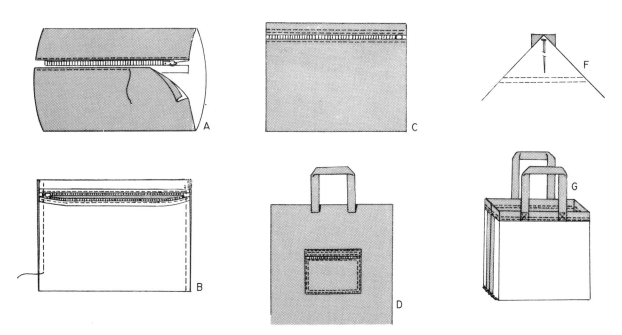

2. Drawstring handbag: Make a pattern and cut a rectangle as directed for the large bag step A. Use laces or cords for drawstrings or make them of self-fabric. Cut 5 cm wide strips twice the length of the rectangle end plus 15 cm for knotting. Fold strips in half wrong sides together; *press*. Turn in raw edges to meet the centre fold; press. *Edge-stitch* the two folded edges together. Trim bag rectangles with appliqué or patch pockets, or make a zipper pocket as explained for the bag, steps A, B, and C. Fold bag, right sides together; *stitch* ends in a 15 mm seam, leaving a 25 mm opening for drawstrings about 56 mm below the upper edges and ending about 25 mm from the bottom fold (A). Press seam open and stitch 6 mm from opening edges (B).

Stitch ends same as for bag, step F. Turn in the top edge 50 mm to form the *casing* for the drawstrings; pin. *Clean-finish* raw edge (if you turn them in 6 mm, make sure they do not cover the openings on the outside of the bag). Stitch inner edge of casing in place. Stitch 6 mm from upper edge of bag, forming a casing (C.). Use a safety pin to guide the drawstrings through casing. Knot drawstring ends together (D).

This style of handbag has been in fashion for hundreds of years. It may be elaborately decorated or made with luxurious fabrics. Make one to fit your lifestyle. This decorated denim bag has a machine-zigzagged appliqué of fabric and lace. It is 25 cm wide, 48 cm long, and 10 cm deep with a patch pocket on the reverse side and has cable cord drawstrings.

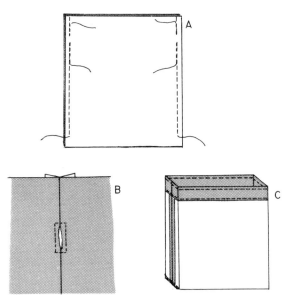

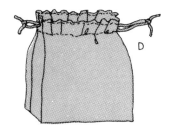

Bands

Strips of self-fabric or contrasting coloured fabric used to finish an edge or set in a garment area as design features.

1. At an edge: Follow the pattern's instructions to prepare the band and *stitch* to the garment. Instead of *slip-stitching* the remaining edge in place, turn in this edge 13 mm and place fold about 3 mm beyond the seam stitching; pin. From the outside stitch in the groove formed where the band joins the garment, catching the remaining edge in the stitching.

2. Set-in Band for a centre front opening: There are no shortcuts to make these beautiful closures. Follow the pattern carefully and do not overhandle the fabric as you work or you may pull the clipped end out of shape.

Baste (basting)

See *machine-baste* and *pin-baste* for quicker basting methods.

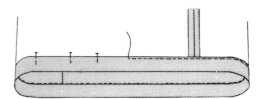

Belt

A strip of fabric or other flexible material that is worn around the body, usually at the waist. Use in a width that will flatter your figure. Test wide belting carefully: more length is needed when belt extends over the rib cage.

1. With buckle: Use your waist measurement plus 17·5 cm. Shape one end of belting, if desired. Cut a fabric strip twice the width of the belting, plus 13 mm. Fold fabric over belting with the wrong side out. Using a zipper foot, *stitch* close to belting, *seam* will be about 6 mm wide (A). Shift seam to centre of belting and *press* seam open being careful not to press creases into the belt edges (B). Pull belt out over shaped end and stitch close to belting. *Trim* seam to 6 mm (C).

Remove belting and turn belt right side out. Do not press. Slip belting into belt fabric, shaped end first by cupping the belting so it is easier to insert (D). Try on belt with buckle. Allow 56 mm for attaching buckle, marking spot where belt goes over the bar. Trim 6 mm from belting. Turn in raw edges, stitch to belt through all thicknesses (E). To make an opening for a prong, stitch a rectangle, as shown, where belt goes over the bar. Make a slash through belt between ends of rectangle (F). *Insert* prong into slash and turn end over bar. Stitch end in place by machine if possible. At shaped end, insert metal eyelets, following manufacturers instructions (G).

Custom-made belts may be made by machine to match all your classic fashions. Select buckles that may be stitched in place for speedy completion.

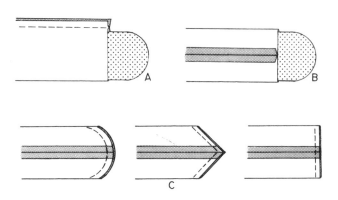

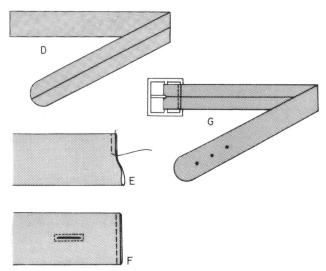

2. With clasp: To make a fabric belt, use belting your waist measurement plus 5 cm. To use decorative elastic purchase the same amount. Make fabric belt same as a Belt With Buckle, steps A, B, and D. Try on belt with clasp, making ends even at both sides. Finish ends as above, step E.

3. Obi tie belt that won't crush: Use 7·5 cm wide belting your waist and/or rib-cage measurement plus 15 cm. For belt, cut a fabric strip 16·3 cm wide the length of the belting plus 13 mm. For tie ends, cut two strips 63 mm wide the length of the belting. To make tie ends, fold strips in half lengthwise. *Stitch* long edges and across one end in a 6 mm *seam. Trim* corner (A). Turn right side out; *press* (B).

Shape belting ends as shown, leaving 25 mm at centre of belting unshaped (C). Fold wide strip of fabric over belting with the wrong sides out. Using a zipper foot, stitch close to straight edge of belting, leaving a 15 cm opening at centre of seam (D). Shift seam to centre of belting and press seam open being careful not to press creases into the belt edges. Pull fabric belt over shaped ends of belting and stitch close to belting, leaving a 25 mm wide opening at each end. Trim shaped seams to 6 mm (E).

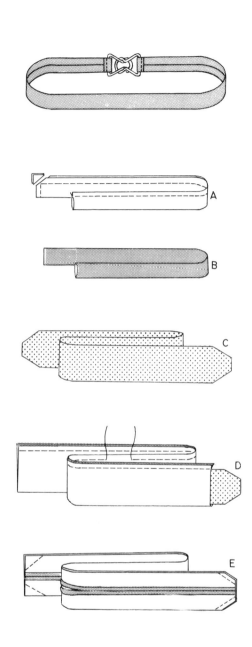

Remove belting. *Insert* tie ends into 25 mm openings, with raw edges even. Stitch securely in place in a 6 mm seam (F). Turn belt right side out through opening. Insert belting through opening in belt, cupping belting for easier insertion. *Slip-stitch* opening edges together (G) using method 2.

Try on belt with shaped ends overlapping at the back and tie ends at front. Mark belt where it rests at your side with a pin. Make a rectangle of zigzag stitches at the mark, making the inside measurement of the rectangle 31 mm long. Make a slit inside the rectangle through all thicknesses (H). Wrap belt around the body, inserting one tie end through opening to the outside. Tie in front (1).

Belt loops
See *Loop* for belt carriers.

Bias
A term used when the fabric weaves (grains) are used diagonally instead of lengthwise or crosswise. Bias cut fabric is used to make binding, cording, facings, and ruffles. Commercial bias tape may be used for most procedures if you do not want to cut your own.

Note: *Knit* fabrics are not cut on the bias. When narrow strips are needed, cut strips the desired width from selvage to selvage as the greater stretch is crosswise.

To cut bias strips straighten only two edges of a large fabric scrap when cutting self-fabric bias. Pull a thread along the lengthwise and the crosswise grain as a cutting guide to form one square corner. Fold fabric corner on a 45-degree angle placing one straight edge on the lengthwise grain and the other straight edge on the crosswise grain: Pin. Cut carefully along the fold. Cut strip the desired width, marking as shown for accurate cutting. (See photograph on page 35.)

Cut opposite ends of each strip on the same slant (A). To join when longer strips are needed *stitch* ends in a 6 mm seam along the straight grain (B). *Press* seam open (C).

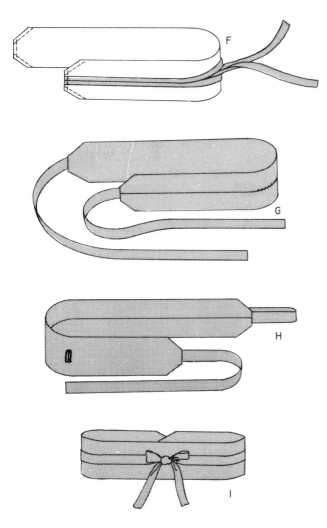

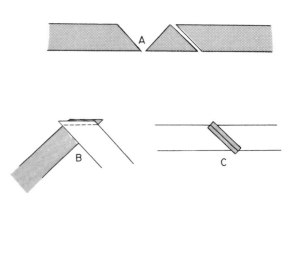

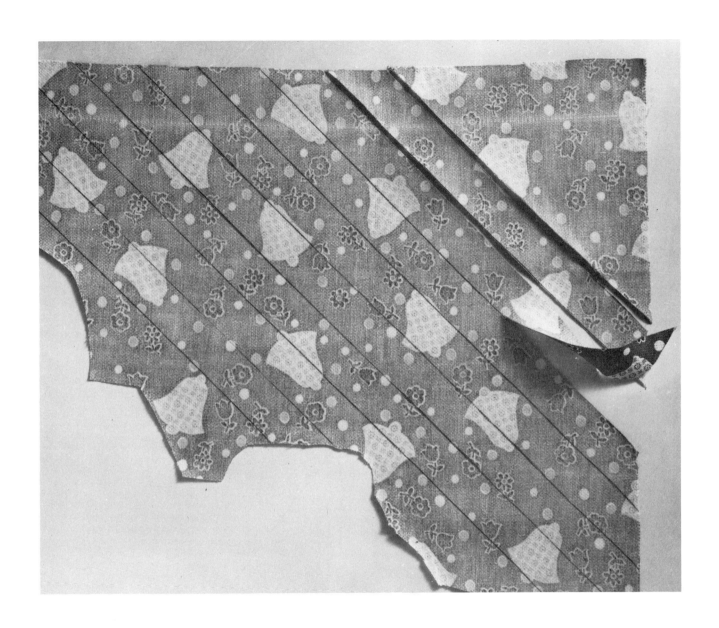

Bias binding

Cut bias strips four times the desired finished width, plus 3 to 6 mm depending on the thickness of the fabric for shaping. Cut strips the length of the edge to be bound, plus 5 cm for finishing ends, piecing as necessary. (Example: for a 6 mm width finished binding, you will need a strip 2·5 cm wide plus 3 to 6 mm for shaping.) *Press* bias strips, stretching gently to remove *slack* (A). Fold strip in half lengthwise; press lightly (B). Open strip, turn in cut edges toward the centre crease, making one side a scant 3 mm wider than the other. Refold along centre crease; press gently (C).

To bind curved edges: The bias strip (self-made or commercial) should be preshaped for best results. Shape binding with steam iron to match the curve of the garment edge. For an inward curve, stretch the two folded edges while easing the single folded edge (D). For an outward curve, stretch the single folded edge, easing the two folded edges (E).

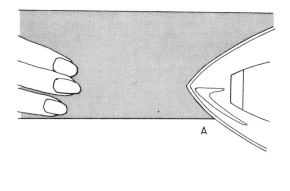

A

B

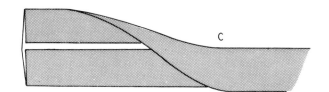

C

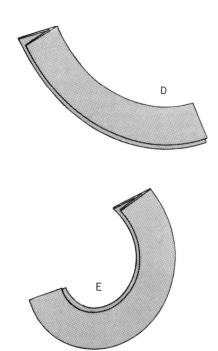

D

E

To bind straight edges, corners, and points pre-shaping is not necessary.

To bind garment edges: Instead of finishing as directed in your commercial pattern, make these simple preparations. For neck, armholes, and hems, the extra fabric layers are not used. Do not cut out facings and interfacings sections for neck and armhole edges, you will need a small hem allowance for adjusting. Establish desired length before binding. To adapt seams, *stitch* 19 mm from raw edge(s) to be bound, then *trim* away the 15 mm seam allowance (A).

For hems, stitch 3 mm from the established hem fold on the garment side. Trim away hem allowance along hemline. For front openings and collars, place interfacing between the two layers of fashion fabric which have been placed wrong sides together. Pin all layers together along edge(s) to be bound. Stitch 19 mm from edge and then trim away 15 mm seam allowance. Before binding an inward corner or V, reinforce, for easy application. Using 20 stitches to 25 mm, stitch 25 mm on each side of the point the same distance from the cut and trimmed edge as the finished width of the binding. *Clip* to stitching (B).

To bind raw edges: Open preshaped binding and pin narrowest edge to the right side of the garment, keeping raw edges even. *Stitch* along crease (A). Turn binding to inside over seam, making sure the folded free edge covers the line of machine stitches. On the outside, stitch in the groove where the binding joins the garment, catching the remaining folded edge in the stitching (B). Note: Use thread that matches the garment.

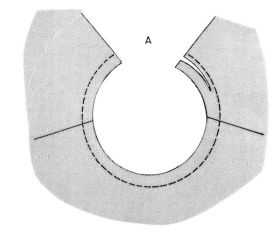

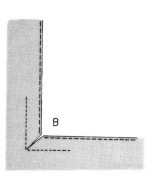

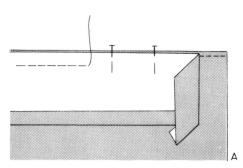

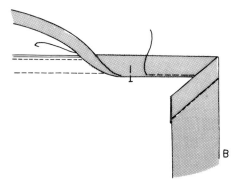

For a continuous edge: To join binding, stitch ends in a seam or lap. For a seam, allow a 25 mm end before starting the *stitching*. When you are within 25 mm of the beginning, break stitching. Fold garment edge so the strip ends are at right angles. Stitch ends on straight grain where they meet (A); *trim* to 6 mm. *Press* seam open; complete stitching.

For a *lapped* joining, turn in one end 13 mm when you start stitching, then extend the remaining end over it 19 mm to complete the lap (B).

To bind corners, points and V's successfully: At an outward corner, end stitches same distance from the corner as the finished binding width; *backstitch* (A). Fold binding diagonally, bring strip up over stitching; make another fold at raw upper edges so strip is on the other side of corner; pin. Stitch binding in place across folds following crease (B).

Turn binding to inside over seam, form a *mitre* on the outside (C). On the inside form another mitre with the folds going in the opposite direction to eliminate bulk; pin (D).

Pin and stitch remaining edge in place same as in step B, to bind raw edges.

At an inward corner or V, spread clipped edges until the reinforcement stitching forms a straight line when stitching binding to garment; stitch on the garment side of the reinforcement stitches so they won't show when binding is completed (E). On the inside, pull fold of mitre through clip (F). Make another mitre with the remaining free edge, having the folds going in the opposite direction to eliminate bulk; pin (G). Pin and stitch remaining edge in place same as step B, to bind raw edges.

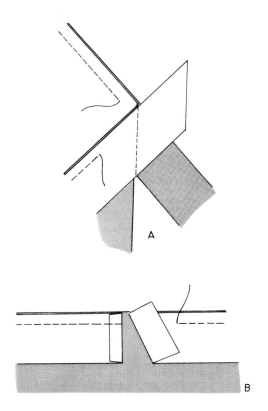

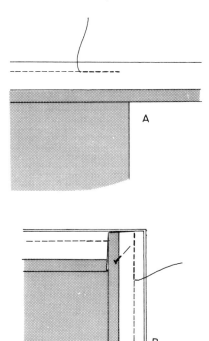

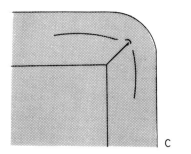

C

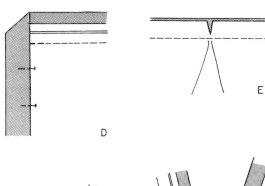

D

E

F

G

Blind-hem stitch

Hemming stitches should be nearly invisible on the outside of the garment and the ridge of the hem should not show through. A blind-hem stitch may be made by machine, following the manufacturer's instructions or it can be made by hand.

Clean-finish the raw edges with a zigzag stitch; stitch and pink or use just a row of stitches 6 mm from the raw edge for knits. Pin hem in place. Turn the hem edge back about 6 mm; take a tiny horizontal stitch through a fibre on the garment and then another on the hem diagonally above the garment stitch. Work back and forth between hem and garment forming zigzag-like stitches between the two layers. Pull up stitches as you *sew*. Every 10–15 cm, stretch the blind-stitches so the stitches are not too tight and secure the thread at this point. The hem will be more durable, and should the thread break, only a short strip will need to be resewn.

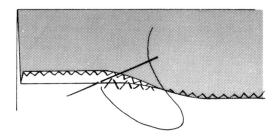

Blousing

1. A term used by designers when extra fabric is needed to allow for fullness on a gathered edge so it will puff out and stand away from the body.

2. The additional length needed when a straight garment is pulled in at the waist with elastic or a drawstring. Allow 2·5–5 cm extra at the waist before cutting out a garment that extends above and below the waist such as a jacket, blouse, dress, or jumpsuit.

Bonded fabrics

See section, A Fast Start.

Buckle closure

See *Belts* type 1 and *Decorative Closures* type 3.

Buttonholes

Slits formed in a garment through which buttons are passed. The classic buttonhole types are the bound, hand-worked, or machine-made. These have been so thoroughly explained so many times that I'm sure you have mastered one or all of them, so now you can add these quick and easy shortcut buttonholes.

1. Slit buttonhole: Make on a completed garment. Determine the length needed, then cut a rectangle 25 mm wide and the length needed for the button plus 19 mm. Fold in half lengthwise; *press* lightly. With right sides together, place crease along buttonhole marking (A) centre and pin (B).

Using 20 stitches to 25 mm, *stitch* 1·5 mm from each side of the crease, *tapering* to a point at each end, taking one stitch across each point. Slash through all thicknesses between the stitching lines, *clipping* each point carefully (C). Turn strip to the inside of the garment; press flat (D). Turn in raw edges to meet the seam allowances of the opening, making sure both sides and ends are the same width; and that all raw edges are covered at each corner; pin. *Edge-stitch* close to folded edges and around the slit (E).

2. Decorative slit buttonhole: Make on a completed garment. Petals, squares, diamonds, and hearts make decorative buttonholes for a simple garment. Determine length of opening needed, then cut out the desired shape, allowing 25 mm beyond the length needed for the button. Fold patch in half; press lightly. On the facing side, place right side of patch down (F). Stitch and slash same as steps A, B, and C above. Turn patch to outside; press. Turn in edges 6 mm; pin in place. Edge-stitch or zigzag folded edge and edge-stitch around slit.

A wool shirtdress is a classic style because of its buttoned front closure with machine-worked buttonholes. The buttons are stitched in place by machine too. Notice the machine-made clasp buckled belt.

C

Casings

Design features, sometimes called tunnels, that use a strip of fabric to form a holder for elastic or a drawstring to pull in fullness close to the body. There are several shortcuts to make elasticized garment areas without using a fabric strip.

The shortcuts as well as the easy classic methods are explained and some types show how to adapt the pattern. Just remember to allow extra length on a sleeve edge if the cuff is eliminated. Allow for blousing on a jacket, blouse, dress, or other garment that will be drawn in close to the waist.

Use soft, densely woven elastic that does not become narrower when stretched. There are some non-roll elastics available for waistlines that hold their width too.

For elasticized waistbands see *Waistband*, methods 3 and 4.

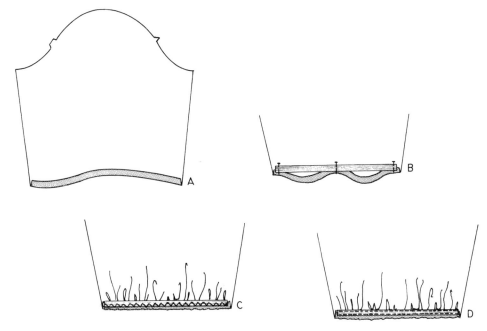

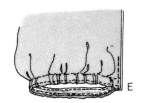

1. Elasticized casing substitutes: Elastic stitched in this manner stretches slightly and does not return to its original length. For sleeves, cut elastic 13 mm less than the wrist measurement. For a waistline (pyjamas, half-slip, etc.), cut elastic 10 cm less than the waist measurement.

To use elastic at an edge, pattern adjustments are not necessary. The 15 mm seam allowance will accommodate elastic as narrow as 6 mm. Turn up the edge 13 mm; *press* (A). Do not be concerned if the raw edge does not lie flat as it will not be noticed when the elastic is *applied*. Cut elastic as directed above. Divide elastic in half for a sleeve or in quarters for a waist, and mark with pins. Pin elastic to garment extending ends 6 mm beyond underarm or side seamlines with the lower edge a scant 3 mm above the fold (B). Note: Leave only one seam unstitched when finishing a waist edge.

Stretch elastic to fit fabric as you *stitch*. Use the widest zigzag stitch (C), or two rows of regulation straight stitches (D). Stitch armhole seam. Fold garment wrong sides together with raw edges even at casing edge. Stitch in a 6 mm seam to about 25 mm above elastic, *back-stitching* at lower edge (E).

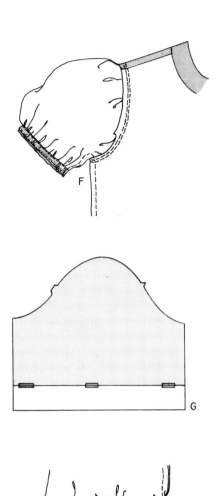

Turn garment with right sides together and stitch side and sleeve seam, starting with a back-stitch at casing and preventing the raw edges from showing at the garment edge (F).

To use elastic to form a ruffle, add the desired finished width of the ruffle to the sleeve below the seamline plus 13 mm for a narrow hem (G). Make narrow hem by turning up edge 13 mm; press. Turn in raw edge and stitch in place. Cut elastic as directed above. Pin and stitch elastic to sleeve as in steps B, C, and D for elastic at an edge. Finish ruffle and casing raw edges as in steps E and F for elastic at an edge (H).

Note: When making toddler's clothes, stitch ends of elastic in place 6 mm from the sleeve side seams. Leave long threads on the machine so you can pull the fabric to start. Make several stitches and ease fabric to fit stretched elastic by making small folds with a pin. Stitch each quarter, arranging the folds as you work.

2. Elasticized self-casing at an edge: The 15 mm seam allowance at a sleeve or garment edge will accommodate 6 mm wide elastic. Simply turn up the edge 15 mm and pin, turn in the raw edge 6 mm. *Stitch* close to the inner folded edge leaving an opening to *insert* elastic. Do not be concerned if the garment side of the casing puckers slightly as it will disappear when the elastic has been inserted (A). If you want to use a wider elastic at the seamline or hemline allow extra length on the pattern the width of the elastic, plus 10 mm. Complete as in step A.

To insert, cut elastic the body measurement. Use a safety pin to pull elastic through casing. Pin remaining end to garment so it won't slide into the casing; make sure the elastic is not twisted (B). *Lap* ends of elastic 13 mm and stitch securely (C). To finish, stretch elastic and stitch remainder of folded edge in place (D).

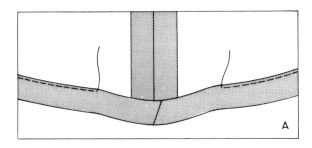

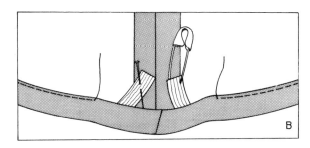

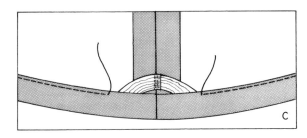

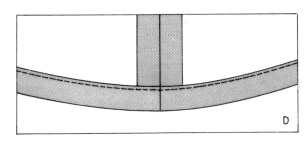

3. Elasticized self-casing with a ruffle: At the pattern's seamline or hemline, add twice the desired finished width of the ruffle, plus the width of the elastic, plus 13 mm (A). (Note: ruffle will make garment section longer, but the elastic will allow for *blousing*, and accommodate the length unless the ruffle is quite deep.)

Stitch garment seams as required. Turn fabric edge to the inside along proposed ruffle fold; pin. *Stitch* ruffle layers together the desired width from fold, overlapping stitches. Turn in raw edge 6 mm; stitch close to folded edge leaving an opening to *insert* elastic (B). Complete as in method 2, steps B, C, and D.

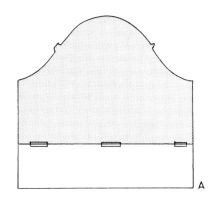

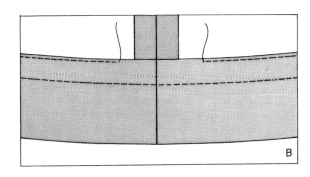

4. Elasticized applied casing at an edge: Use commercial single-fold or wide bias tape or a straight strip of fabric the width of the elastic plus 19 mm. For the fabric strip, turn in both long edges 6 mm and press (A). At the garment edge, trim seam or hem allowance to 10 mm; turn up and press. Pin casing over pressed garment edge 3 mm above the fold, as shown, turning in the ends 6 mm where they meet. (This opening will be used to insert the elastic.) *Stitch* close to both folded edges of the casing through all thicknesses (B). Insert elastic as in method 2, steps B and C. *Stitch* ends of casing in place as shown (C).

5. Elasticized applied casing with a ruffle: At the pattern's seamline or hemline, add the width of the ruffle plus 10 mm for a narrow hem (A).

Stitch garment seams as required. Make a narrow hem at garment edge by turning in raw edges 4·5 mm and then again 4·5 mm: stitch folded edge in place. Prepare a straight strip as in method 4, step A or use commercial single-fold wide or narrow bias tape for casing strips. Place one pressed edge of strip along seamline or hemline (the distance from the narrow hem edge will be the same as you allowed for the ruffle); pin, turning in the ends 6 mm where they meet. Stitch close to both pressed edges (B). *Insert* elastic through opening where the turned in ends meet as in method 2, steps B and C and stitch ends same as method 4, step C.

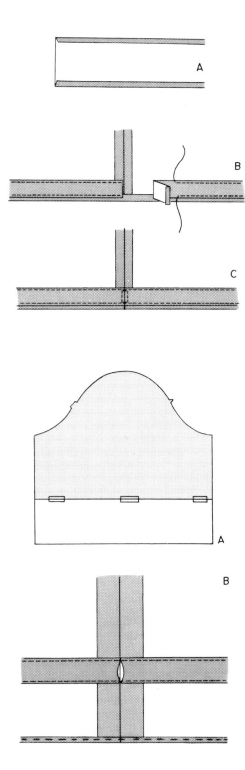

6. Elasticized applied casing at waistline: Stitch garment seams as required. Prepare a straight strip of fabric as in method 4 step A or use commercial single-fold wide or narrow bias tape. For a continuous casing, centre strip over waist marking, pin, turning in ends where they meet 6 mm. *Stitch* close to both pressed edges (A). *Insert* elastic as in method 2, steps B and C and method 4 step C (B).

For a waistline casing that ends at a zipper opening, *apply* casing strip, steps A and B, ending casing at seamline (C). After *inserting* elastic, *stitch* it securely in place where the zipper stitching will fall (D).

For a waistline casing that ends at facing edges, apply casing, steps A and B, turning in ends 13 mm (E). The elastic should be the waist measurement, less the distance across the garment, when closed, that will not be gathered by the elastic. After inserting elastic, stitch it securely in place (F).

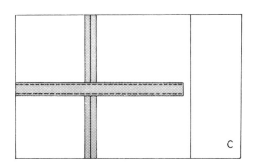

C

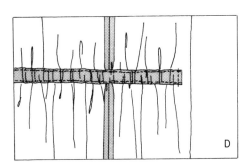

D

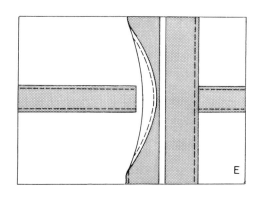

E

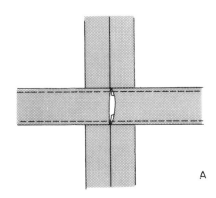

A

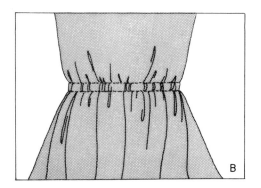

B

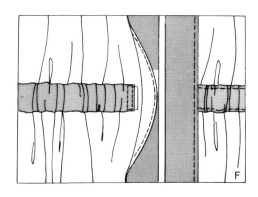

F

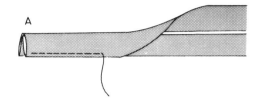

7. Drawstring casings: Cable cord, shoe laces, ribbon, or self-fabric strips make the best drawstring. To make a fabric drawstring, cut a straight strip four times the desired finished width. The length should be the measurement of the garment where the drawstring will be used, plus at least 30 cm so the ends will not pull into the casing. Fold strip in half lengthwise, wrong sides together; press. Open fold and turn in long raw edges to meet crease; press. *Stitch* close to both folded edges (A).

Before applying the casing, openings must be made on the outside or in a *seam* in order to *insert* the drawstring. For openings on a garment, use *slit*, machine-made or hand-worked buttonholes or metal eyelets (follow manufacturer's instructions for insertion). Reinforce area with an iron-on patch or *fuse* on a self-fabric patch on the wrong side. Make sure these openings will accommodate your drawstring.

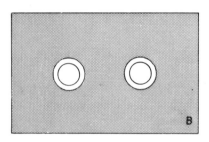

Make opening as shown, between proposed placement of casing (B).

Stitch casing in place (C), selecting the appropriate type from the elasticized methods 4, 5, and 6. Insert drawstring through one opening on the outside with safety pin or the metal lacer on the shoe string and pull out the drawstring through the remaining opening (D). Form a knot at each end of drawstring or narrow hem ribbon ends. To prevent drawstrings from pulling out of casing, stitch across centre back of garment through casing and drawstring (E).

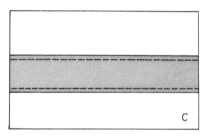

For an opening in a seam, stitch seam above and below proposed casing placement, *backstitching* at both points (F). Stitch casing in place selecting the appropriate type from the elasticized methods 4, 5, and 6. Insert drawstring as in step D.

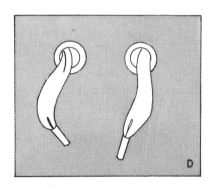

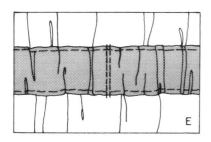

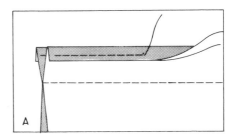

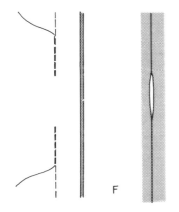

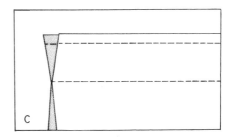

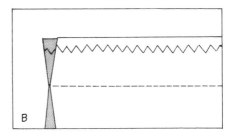

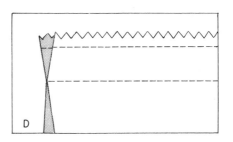

Clasp buckle

See *Belt* method 2 and *Decorative closures*, method 2.

Clean-Finish (Neatening)

To finish the free, raw edge of a facing, hem, or other fabric section. To clean-finish an edge, turn under 6 mm and stitch (A) or zigzag (B).

For knits stitch 6 mm from edge (C). For tightly woven, non-fraying fabrics stitch 6 mm from edge and pink (D). Another method is to lap lace 6 mm over edge; stitch and then turn in end 13 mm where it laps over starting end (E).

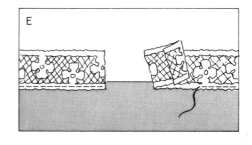

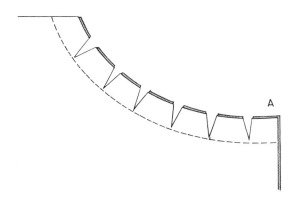

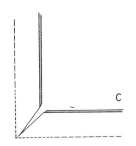

Clip (clipping)

Short snips made in seam allowance after a seam is stitched or when a garment section is *reinforced*. Clip just to the line of stitching, but not through stitches so seam allowances will lie flat or to allow for special handling. Clip *inward* curves at even intervals (A).

To test if you have clipped enough, hold fabric at each end; you should be able to pull it in a straight line (B). If seam allowance curls, more clips are needed. Clip reinforced *inward* corners to line of *reinforcement stitches* (C).

Closures

Openings that allow a garment to be slipped on and off easily need fastenings to keep the openings shut when being worn. There are many types available. Choose closures that enhance the garment and are still easy to attach. See general title: *Buttonholes* with buttons, *Decorative closures, Hooks and eyes, Snaps, Tape fastener, Tie closures, Zipper.*

Collar

A finished band of fabric that is stitched to the neck edge. Collars are often the crowning glory of a garment and must be finished with expertise to be complementary. The instructions given with your pattern are usually adequate and are expected to accommodate all fabrics. Here are the basics:

Every collar has two layers of fashion fabric—the layer that is seen is called the uppercollar; the layer next to the garment is the undercollar—and a layer of interfacing.

Construction Tips: For some tightly woven or knitted fabrics, the *interfacing* may be omitted, this is called an *unstructured* collar. For quick application, interfacing is *machine-basted* or *fused* to the undercollar. Mark corners or points. Trim away interfacing about 3 mm beyond the marking before positioning to eliminate bulky lumps (A). Machine-baste a scant 15 mm from the cut edge (B). Before fusing interfacing in place, trim a scant 15 mm from all edges (C). For a collar with a folded edge, cut as directed. Extend interfacing 10 mm over foldline and stitch in place on the undercollar side of the foldline (D).

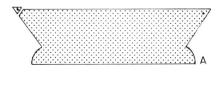

A

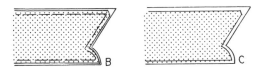

B   C

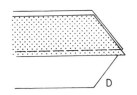

D

E

F

G

When stitching a collar that encircles the neck in one piece, *stitch* from one neck edge to the centre back and break stitching; then stitch from the opposite side of the neck edge to the centre over-lapping the stitches (E). This will make the collar lie evenly on both sides of the garment. Use *reinforcement* stitches at corners and points. *Trim, grade, clip,* and/or *notch* the seam allowances.

To prevent the undercollar from showing, there are several quick and easy procedures to follow. For lightweight fabrics, when pinning collar sections together, first pin the neck edges together, then pin the uppercollar edges a scant 3 mm inside the undercollar edges. The uppercollar will bubble slightly. *Stitch* collar sections together 15 mm from raw undercollar edges, easing uppercollar to fit (F).

For medium and heavy weight fabrics, make a 3–6 mm deep dart at the centre of the uppercollar; pin. Pin neck edges of collar together. With uppercollar on top, shape collar as it looks in the pattern envelope's sketch. Pin uppercollar in place where it falls. Stitch collar sections together 15 mm from raw undercollar edges, easing uppercollar to fit (G).

To *favour* the uppercollar, when collar is turned right side out, some pressing is needed. After *trimming* the seam allowances, turn the undercollar clipped seam allowances over the interfacing; *press* flat (H). Turn collar right sides out, carefully shaping corners or points. Press, favouring uppercollar.

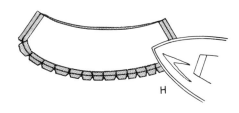

H

Collar neck edges seldom ever match the shape of garment neck edge so it will save time and temper if you *reinforce* the garment neck edge. *Stitch* from centre front to centre back on one side, break stitches and then stitch from centre front to centre back on the other side overlapping the stitches (1). *Clip* to stitching at even intervals.

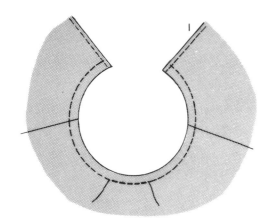

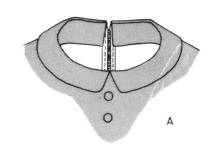

1. Flat two-piece collar: When the collar has been shaped and favoured properly according to the fabric, follow the pattern's sewing guide for construction (A).

2. Band collar: These collars can be narrow, wide, or folded over like a turtleneck and may be cut on the straight or bias grain. Prepare collar and *stitch* to neck edge as directed on the pattern, *pressing* seam toward collar. Pin collar along fold. (For a turtleneck, pin both folds in place.) For light- or medium-weight fabric, turn in raw edge about 13 mm so it just covers the stitching at neckline; pin, catching only enough fabric to hold edge in place. From the outside, stitch in the groove formed where the collar joins the garment through all thicknesses, catching the turned-in edge in the stitching (B).

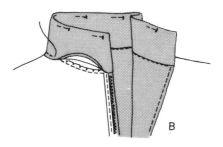

For heavy fabrics, trim seam allowances to 6 mm beyond the stitching; zigzag the trimmed edge. Pin in place over seam. From the outside, stitch in the groove formed where the collar joins the garment through all thicknesses, catching in zigzag edge in the stitching (C).

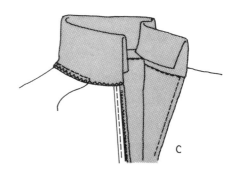

3. Classic shirt collar: The neckband may be a separate pattern piece or it may be cut as part of the collar. Prepare as directed by pattern, using the construction tips for a quick and easy, good-looking collar. For the collar with separate neckband, pin and *stitch* undercollar (interfaced) side of the band to the shirt. *Trim* and *grade* seam (A). *Press* seam toward band. Turn in remaining edge so it just covers the stitching; pin. *Edge-stitch* in place, continuing around all edges of the band (B).

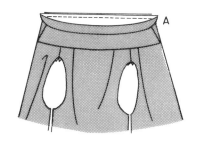

For the collar and band combination, pin and *stitch* undercollar (interfaced) side to garment. *Trim* and *grade* seam (C). *Press* seam toward collar. Turn in remaining edge so it just covers the stitching; pin. *Edge-stitch* in place (D). You may continue the edge-stitching around all the collar edges, if desired. It will reinforce the edges.

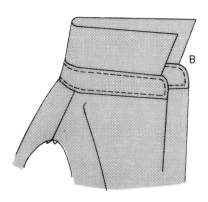

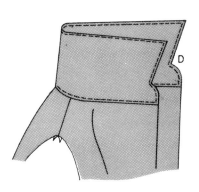

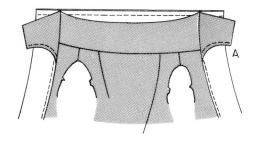

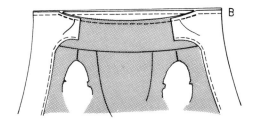

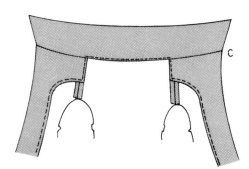

4. Collar with lapels (folded front facing): Prepare collar according to your pattern, shaping and favouring collar as explained in the construction tips. Omit the back neck facing if included. *Clean-finish* inner and shoulder edge of facing. *Stitch* facing to symbol. Pin and stitch undercollar (interfaced side) to garment, keeping facing free (A). Pin and stitch uppercollar to facing (B).

Trim and *clip* seam allowances, clipping to stitching alongside the shoulder seam. *Press* front neck seams open and press back neck seam toward collar between shoulder seams. Turn in remaining collar edge so it just covers the seam; pin. Also pin shoulder edges of facing in place. Stitch across facing, following the shoulder seam; *pivot* and *edge-stitch* back neck edge; pivot and stitch remaining facing edge in place (C).

5. Collar with lapels (stitched facing seam): At this time, we break a tailoring rule and apply the interfacing to the uppercollar and the front facing instead of the undercollar and garment front. After interfacing is positioned, pin and *stitch* undercollar to garment between symbols. Trim seam allowances and clip garment neck edge. Press seam open.

Stitch facings together and *clean-finish* inner edge. Stitch uppercollar to facing neck edge between symbols. Don't trim the seam allowances, press open, clipping facing where necessary so it will lie flat.

Place uppercollar and facing over undercollar and garment, with right sides together. Match neck seams; pin and then baste them together. Turn garment wrong side out with the uppercollar and facing on top. Shape collar and lapels to look like the pattern envelope's sketch.

When the collar and lapels are shaped satisfactorily, the uppercollar and facing raw edges will not meet the raw edges of the undercollar and garment. Pin collar and lapel edges together where they fall. Now shape the jacket and facing edges below the lapel so the facings won't show when the garment is buttoned. Pin these edges together.

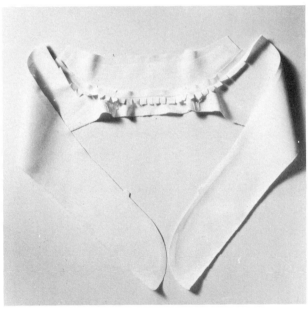

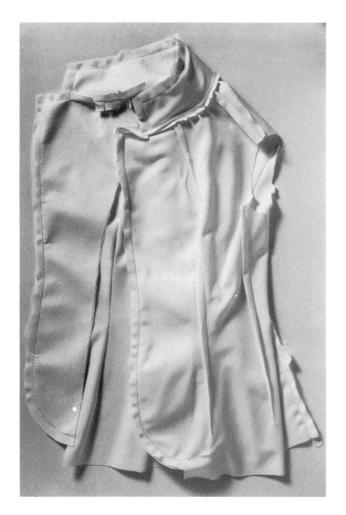

Stitch collar sections together between symbols, 15 mm from raw undercollar edges easing or stretching so the layers will fit. Stitch facing to garment, between symbols and lower edge, 15 mm from raw garment edge, easing or stretching as necessary. *Trim, grade, clip,* and *notch* seam allowances as needed.

Press facing seam allowance over itself to top buttonhole marking. Press garment seam allowance over the interfacing between buttonhole marking and collar. Press undercollar seam allowance over interfacing.

Turn collar right sides out and facing to inside; press. Match neck and shoulder seams; pin. Stitch in groove formed by the seam and complete garment.

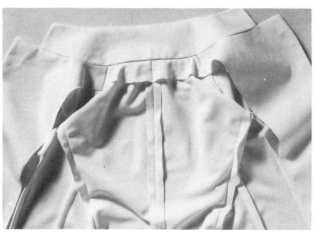

Corduroy
See section, A Fast Start.

Crisp fabrics
Fabric that stands away from the body, holding the silhouette of the design. Crisp fabrics fall in rounded folds that spread at the lower edge of a garment unless the fabric is controlled by pressing. Crisp fabrics make great sharp pleats when pressed. Organdie, linen, voile, and gabardine, are some of the classic types of crisp fabrics.

Cuff

A band of fabric stitched to the lower edge of a sleeve or pant leg, or an extension of a sleeve or pant leg folded back over itself. See *Pants hems*. Commercial patterns give classic instructions that are meant to accommodate any fabric. For some easy shortcuts to make cuffs in a hurry, read on!

Most cuffs are cut with a folded outer edge. Some styles may be stitched to the sleeve while it is flat but most are stitched in place after the sleeve is joined to the garment and the underarm seam has been stitched.

Construction tips: Each cuff has two layers of fashion fabric and a layer of interfacing. For tightly woven or knitted fabric the interfacing may be omitted. This is called an *unstructured* cuff. For speedier application, the interfacing is *machine-basted* or *fused* to the notched edge of the cuff. Mark corners or points on double-layered cuffs. *Trim* away interfacing about 3 mm beyond the marking before positioning to eliminate lumps at the corners or points. For cuffs with a foldline, place interfacing 10 mm over foldline. To *machine-baste*, stitch a scant 15 mm from the raw fabric edges. Then stitch alongside the foldline on the unnotched side of the cuff (A). To fuse, trim ends to a scant 15 mm and place the long edge about 13 mm from the notched edge (B).

For a double-layered cuff, trim corners and machine-baste a scant 15 mm from all edges (C). To fuse, trim away all edges a scant 15 mm then attach (D). When stitching, use *reinforcement stitches* at corners and points *Trim, grade,* and *clip* or *notch* seam allowances. If your sleeve has the new straight opening and the cuff has an extension, *pivot* at symbol and *stitch* to raw edge. *Clip* to corner stitching when *trimming* the seam allowances (E). *Apply* cuff as shown in method 2, page 59.

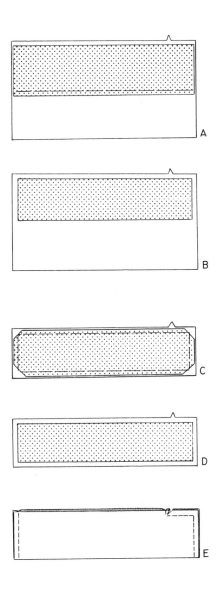

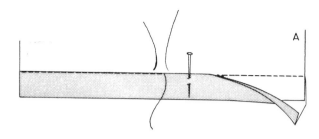

A

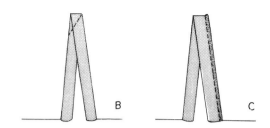

B

C

The classic sleeve openings used with a cuff are the continuous lap and the faced straight edge that are made on the sleeve while it is still flat. To use a continuous lap, follow the pattern's instructions for slashing and stitching the 5 cm wide strip to sleeve. *Press* strip away from sleeve. Turn in remaining long edge 10 mm and pin over stitching. *Stitch* in groove formed where the strip is joined to the sleeve, catching in the folded edge in the stitching (A). Fold lap in half at top of opening and stitch the folds together diagonally as shown (B). A selvage edge may be used instead. Cut the strip 3 cm wide and pin edge 3 mm over the stitching. Complete same as step B for the turned-under edge (C).

For a straight edge opening, *stitch* a 5 by 7·5 cm strip to the right side as shown, *pivoting* at symbols. *Trim* to within 6 mm of stitching and *clip* to corner stitches (D). Turn strip to the inside; *press*. Turn in raw edges 6 mm and *edge-stitch* in place (E). Note: This step may be eliminated. See method 2, opposite.

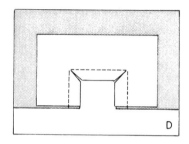

D

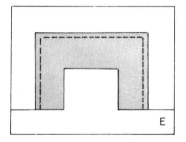

E

1. Classic cuff: Prepare cuff and sleeve edge and *stitch* together along the notched edge. *Trim* and *grade* seam allowances. *Press* seam toward cuff. Turn in remaining raw edge 13 mm and cover stitching about 3 mm; pin just deep enough to hold fabric in place (A). Turn sleeve wrong side out. From the outside, stitch in the groove where cuff joins sleeve, catching all layers in stitching (B).

For bulky fabric, trim remaining edge to 6 mm and zigzag. Place edge 6 mm beyond stitching; pin. Stitch in place as in step B for the turned in edge (C).

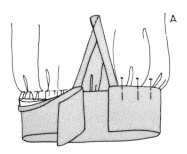 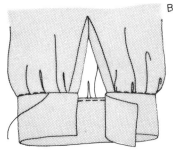 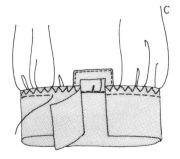

2. Straight edge opening with classic cuff: This is the quickest method and it is suitable for all fabrics. Prepare cuff and stitch extension (if given) as shown above in construction tips, for step E. Pin raw edges of cuff together. Buttonholes may be made now. Add *gathering-threads* or make *pleats*. Pin cuffs, to sleeve, placing finished edges at symbols, adjusting any gathers smoothly. Stitch cuff to sleeve. Zigzag all raw edges together (A) Or stitch 3 mm from raw edges to help prevent fraying. Turn cuff down; press seam toward sleeve. *Edge-stitch* cuff and 13 mm from raw edges to hold them in place (B). Complete cuff.

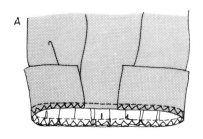  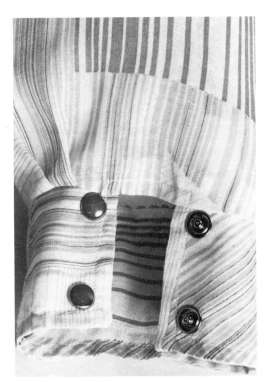

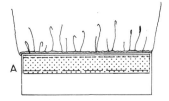

A

3. Band cuff: There are two quick and easy shortcuts to apply this type of cuff. To stitch cuff to sleeve while it is flat, attach interfacing and make *gathering-threads*. Pin cuff to sleeve; adjust gathers and stitch seam (A). *Stitch* armhole seam. Then stitch the underarm, side, and cuff seams in one operation (B). Turn up cuff along foldline; pin. Turn in remaining raw edge 13 mm and place about 3 mm beyond seam stitching; pin just deep enough to hold layers together (C). Turn garment wrong sides out.

From the outside, stitch in groove where cuff joins sleeve (D). For bulky fabrics, trim raw edge to 6 mm and zigzag. Place edge 6 mm over stitching. Pin and stitch in place same as step C for the turned in edge (E).

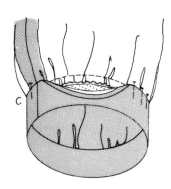

B

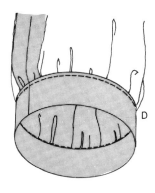

D

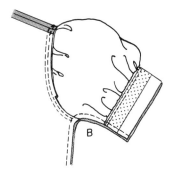

C

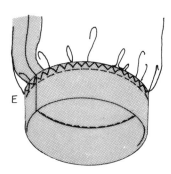

E

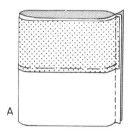

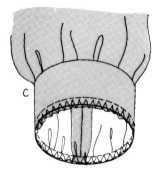

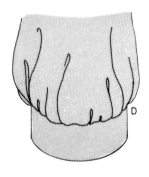

To stitch band to sleeve in a circle: Attach interfacing and stitch cuff seam (A). Fold cuff wrong
sides together; *press* (B). Add gathering-threads
to sleeve. Pin cuff to sleeve, adjust gathers, and
stitch seam. Zigzag raw edges (C). A row of
straight stitches 3 mm away may be used to help
prevent fraying. Turn cuff down (D).

For a turned-up band cuff, prepare cuff as in
steps A and B above. Pin and stitch cuff to wrong
side of the sleeve. *Trim* seam allowances to 6 mm
and zigzag (A). Turn cuff to outside covering seam
(B).

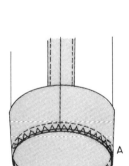

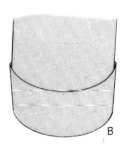

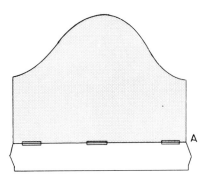

4. Cuff cut-in-one with sleeve: To make a 25 mm wide cuff add 7 cm to sleeve pattern at hemline or seamline. Fold up pattern as the cuff will be positioned and trim ends even with underarm cutting line (A). *Clean-finish* raw edges of sleeve. *Stitch* armhole seam. Then stitch cuff, sleeve, and underarm seam in one operation (B). Turn up sleeve edge 4·5 cm; press. Stitch hem in place about 6 mm from *clean-finished* edge (C). Turn up folded edge; press (D).

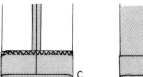

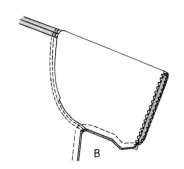

5. Simulated cuff: This cuff is found most often on men's short-sleeve shirts. Turn back sleeve hem on pattern piece. Draw a line 6 mm below where the inner edge falls. Cut along this line and add 13 mm length to the sleeve (A). After sleeves are cut out, turn up hem allowance; press (B). Turn this pressed edge up along the raw hem edge; press.

Stitch 6 mm from second pressed edge through all thicknesses (C). Stitch sleeve in armhole seam. Stitch sleeve and side seam in a *flat-felled* seam, in one continuous operation (D).

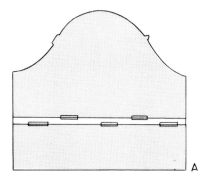

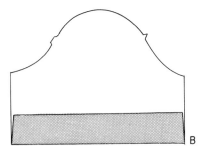

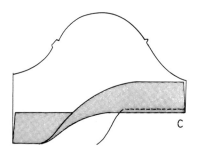

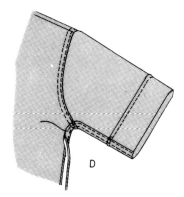

Curved seams

These are used for both structural and enclosed seams. See *Seams*.

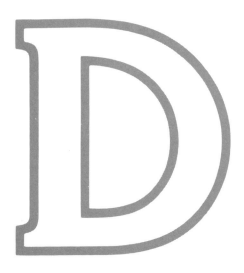

D

Decorative closures

When you are tired of the traditional closings, invent some of your own. There are a wide variety of buttons, buckles, and clasps that make novel closures. Decorative closures may be used on a garment that just meets at the centre front or a lapped closing that has had the right front modified.

To change a garment with a lapped closure, cut out as instructed by pattern. Turn back the front and facing pattern pieces leaving 15 mm beyond the centre front marking; pin. For a woman, modify the right front only; for a man the left front only and cut away excess garment and facing fabric. Complete garment as usual, stitching along the centre front for the modified edge.

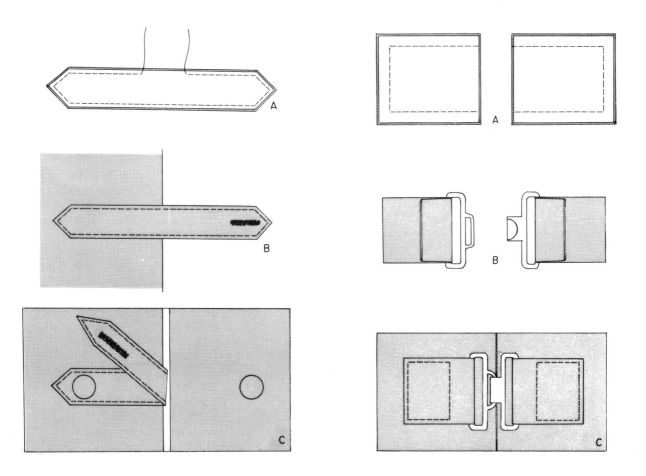

1. Tab closure: Make fabric strip as wide and as long as needed to accommodate buttons plus 6 mm seam allowance on all edges. For soft fabrics, be sure to use interfacing. Make a pattern for the desired shape, cutting two fabric sections for each tab to be used. *Stitch* long edges and ends, leaving an opening to turn right side out (A). *Trim* corners, points, and curves. Turn through opening; press. Sew opening using *slip-stitch* method 2. Make a *buttonhole* in one end. On one garment edge matching centre fronts, top-stitch 3–6 mm from all edges, stitching tab in place (B). Sew buttons to one end of tab and at opposite of opening (C).

2. Clasp closure: Fabric strips should be as wide as the clasp's bar when finished. Make a pattern to find out how long and wide a finished strip is needed with a turn back long enough to allow machine application; add a 6 mm seam allowance to all edges. Cut four fabric sections for each clasp fastener. *Stitch* two fabric sections together along both long edges and one end (A). *Trim* corners, points, and curves. Turn right side out; press.

Slip raw ends over bar and pin to strip about 13 mm from finished end (B). Pin to garment with centre fronts meeting. Adjust strips if necessary, trimming away excess. Stitch in place making sure raw ends are turned in so they won't show (C).

3. Belt closure: Make a pattern to see how long the strip should be, allowing 13 mm extra to turn in raw ends. Make same as *belt* with buckle, method 1. Substituting interfacing, if needed, for belting. Fasten buckle and eyelet end and pin to garment with centre fronts matching. Turn in raw ends 13 mm and pin securely in place. *Stitch* strips in place close to edges and across ends near opening edges.

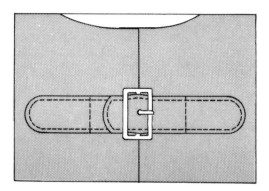

Decorative slit buttonhole

Instructions are found under *buttonholes*, method 2.

Design repeats (sometimes called pattern repeats). Some fabrics are woven or printed along their length with the designs repeated at even intervals. In order to *match* the designs at the seams, additional fabric must be purchased. Measure the exact length of the repeat. Examine the pattern layout to see how the garment pieces are placed and count the number of repeats needed. Multiply the number of repeats by the length of one repeat and then add this figure to your fabric requirements.

Directional stitching

An instructive direction to remind you to stitch with the grain of the fabric. Always *stitch* from the widest part of the garment to the narrowest. Stitch all seams in the same direction. Have you ever made a gored skirt where several of the seams curled or dipped, and wondered why? Chances are that you stitched from the hem to the waist edge on the good, smooth seams and stitched from the waist edge to the hem edge on the unsatisfactory, puckered seams. Stitching against the grain will often cause the seams to stretch.

Drawstrings

Instructions for making drawstrings and their casings are found under *casings*, method 6.

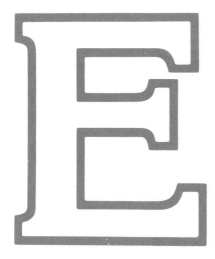

E

Ease (easing)

There are several definitions of ease that are used in conjunction with sewing.

1. Wearing ease: The extra amount of circumference and/or length added to the pattern so you can sit, stretch, bend, and walk comfortably after the garment is stitched together.

2. Ease as a sewing term: Design features sometimes require a smooth seam, but extra fabric is needed along one side of the seam to cup smoothly over the bust, shoulders, or hips. To accomplish this, one garment section is made longer along the seamline than along the seamline of the section to which it will be stitched.

To stitch a seam with a small amount of extra fabric, pin sections together, matching symbols. Divide the excess fabric equally, placing pins about 6 mm apart. Stretch the smaller section slightly as you stitch, working in the excess fabric so it cups smoothly, without puckers, along the stitching.

If the fabric is stiff or heavy, or if there is an excessive amount of fabric to be eased in such as for a sleeve cap, an *ease-thread* is needed (see instructions below) to stitch a seam without a pucker.

Ease-threads

To add an ease-thread for *easing*, use slightly longer stitches and loosen the top tension several points—the heavier the fabric the longer the ease-stitches should be. *Stitch* from the right side of the fabric a scant 15 mm from the raw edge so the stitches won't show on the outside of the garment and so you can pull the bobbin thread (it pulls the easiest). Return tension and stitch length to the correct points.

Edge-stitch

A row of machine-stitches used to hold a finished edge in place. Stitch close to a garment, opening, or pocket edge through all thicknesses—usually 1·5 mm.

Elasticized casings

Self or applied, with or without ruffles or at a waistline are explained under *casings*, methods 1 to 6.

Enclosed seams

These form a finished edge for collars, cuffs, and other garment appendages and require special handling to ensure a smooth edge when the two fabric layers and often a layer of interfacing are turned over the seam allowances. To stitch, see *seams*. For handling techniques see *trim, clip*, and *pressing*.

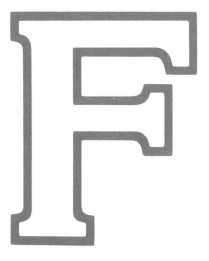

F

Face
A term used to direct you to use a facing to complete a garment edge.

Facing
A layer of fabric on the inside of a garment, stitched to the edge to protect the garment and cover the raw edges or folded to the inside. Inner free edges are *clean-finished*. Note: There are many finishes such as bias binding and bias facings that may be substituted for a facing. See *armhole* and *neck facings, hems,* and *sleeves.*

Fashion fabric
The fabric used for the major portion of the garment, not the interfacing, lining, or other fabrics used to complete the garment.

Fastener
Any type of gadget used to close a garment. See *buttonholes, decorative closures, hooks and eyes, snaps, tape fastener, tie closures,* and *zipper.*

Favour

Extension of outer layer of fabric slightly beyond the seam stitching so that the underneath layer does not show on the outside of a garment when it is worn.

Finger press

To force seams open with the fingers and then press them flat by drawing a thumbnail or other flat, blunt object along the stitching.

Flat-felled seam

Stitch garment sections, wrong sides together in a seam (A). *Press* seam allowances in the same direction. *Trim* the lower seam allowance to 3 mm. Turn in remaining seam allowance to meet the trimmed edge and edge-stitch in place (B). Note: For garments made of heavier fabrics, you may need a wider seam allowance on top in order to turn in the top one and have enough fabric for a good-looking seam. Place one edge 25 mm from the other and stitch 6 mm from the short edge. Trim the short edge to 3 mm and complete same as above.

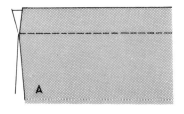

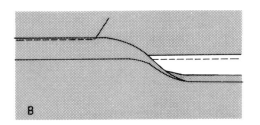

Foldover braid

A decorative trim used in place of bias binding. It is a quick and easy way to finish edges of heavier fabric when made up in garments such as jackets, skirts, and capes. Simply slip the braid over the raw edges with the longest fold underneath. Stitch in place through all thicknesses. To *mitre* corners and points, see *bias binding.*

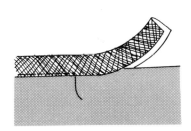

French seam substitute

Use for sheers or fabrics that ravel easily. Stitch the seam, but do not press seam allowance open. Turn in raw edges to meet the seam and then stitch them together. Also recommended for men's wear.

French tack substitute

Cut a 7·5 cm strip of seambinding and fold in half. *Edge-stitch* woven edges together. *Insert* strips into hem of lining as it is stitched in place. Then *tack* the binding to the garment hem.

Fusibles (fuse)

Heat-sensitive fabric or a fusing material that is used to bond two layers of fabric together. Follow manufacturer's instructions. Be sure to test a scrap of fabric to make sure it will not be damaged by the heat required to fuse the fabric layers together. Iron-on patches and interfacing are fusibles. Fusible material may also be bought in narrow or wide strips and as a spray-on substance.

The fusing agents are great time-savers: fuse hems, facings, interfacing, appliqués, trims, and anything else that can be secured safely on your fabric.

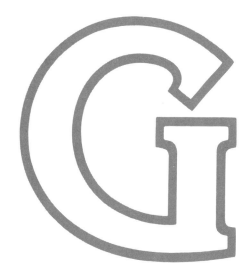

G

Gathering-threads

To add gathering-threads use the longest machine stitch and loosen the top tension several points. For firmly woven, medium to heavy fabrics, use a heavier thread on the bobbin. Use two rows of threads for smooth gathers. Place the first row a scant 15 mm from the raw edge and another row 6 mm away in the seam allowance. *Stitch* from the right side of the fabric when joining in a seam. Stitch from the wrong side of a ruffle that is to be applied.

Gathers

Soft folds of fabric formed by drawing up fabric with *gathering-threads* before the *seam* is *stitched*.

Grade (grading)

To grade seam allowances of an enclosed seam, trim away excess fabric, which will cause bulk when the section is turned right side out. Trim the seam allowances into graduated width layers. Trim away *interfacing* caught in the seam close to the stitching. Trim the top seam allowance to 3 mm and the bottom layer to 6 mm. See *clip, notch,* and *trim* techniques used with grading.

Grain

Woven fabrics have two sets of threads interwoven at right angles. The threads that run up and down in the same direction as the selvages are called the lengthwise grain. The threads that run back and forth between the selvages are called the crosswise grain. Be sure the fabric you like has been woven on true grain. The selvages should be straight and smooth with the lengthwise threads parallel to the selvages and the crosswise threads should run parallel to each other at right angles to the lengthwise threads from selvage to selvage. Examine the fabric carefully before purchasing—it may be on true grain for one half of the width to the fold and be off-grain on the other half. Your garment may not hang evenly on both sides when completed if off-grain fabric is used. Off-grain printed fabrics will be more obvious as the design will not run parallel to the crosswise threads.

H

Hand-sewing

The oldest sewing method. The cave man sewed skins together with bone needles and narrow leather strips. There are some sewing procedures that only hand-sewing will give you the best results.

A *blind-stitched* hem or facing held in place with carefully made hand-sewn stitches, that are not visible on the outside of the garment, is the goal of every seamstress and tailor. *Slip-stitching* is another hand-sewn technique that cannot be replaced by a machine. The *back-stitch* was used for a durable seam before the sewing machine was invented. There are other hand-sewing stitches used by designers to make their one-of-a-kind original garments that you may have used to make a special garment.

Hem (hems)

A strip of fabric folded under the outer garment layer and then *stitched* or *sewn* in place. Today's wash-and-wear fabrics need a quick and easy hem that may be stitched in place. Nearly any traditional hem may be machine-blindstitched in place; simply follow the instructions given in your sewing machine manual. The type of machine-stitched hem used should be matched to the type and style of garment. Even a "designer" dress will look great with a stitched hem, if it is a continuation of *top-stitching* used on the front openings. Cape and coat hems are also stitched in place by designers when using heavy woollens. Use tightly woven or knitted fabric. Wider hems may be stitched or fused in place, and trims may be used to finish off an edge in place of a hem. Before turning up a hem, the raw edge must be *clean-finished:* Zigzag or stitch 6 mm from raw edge and pink woven fabrics. Knits need only a row of stitches 6 mm from the raw edge. For sheers and other lightweight fabrics, turn under 13 mm for durability. Make hem allowance adjustments on pattern before cutting, or trim to recommended width after the hem is turned up.

1. Easy narrow hem: Use a 15 mm wide hem. *Clean-finish* raw edges if necessary. *Pin-baste* hem in place. *Press*, removing pins and easing in any fullness. *Stitch* a scant 6 mm from fold and again 6 mm away (A). Second row of stitches should be about 6 mm from the clean finished edge.

2. Easy wide hem: Sheer fabric looks well with a single row of stitching and a 13 mm turn-under. Other fabrics should have two rows. For sheers make hem 7·5–12·5 cm deep and *stitch* in place (B). For other fabrics make hem 2·5–5 cm depending on the fullness. Stitch 6 mm from inner edge of hem and again 6 mm away (C).

A stable double-knit garment does not require a finish for the raw edge of the hem. Simply stitch hem in place with one or two rows of stitching that matches any top-stitching if it is used.

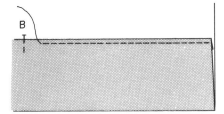

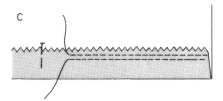

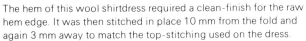

The hem of this wool shirtdress required a clean-finish for the raw hem edge. It was then stitched in place 10 mm from the fold and again 3 mm away to match the top-stitching used on the dress.

Make a durable top-stitched hem for your next wrap skirt. A 25 mm finished hem with a 13 mm turnunder was used for both the lower edge and the opening facing edges with a *mitre*, method 1, at the corners. The inner folded edge was stitched in place and then stitched again 13 mm away.

3. Fused hem: Narrow strips of fusible material or sprays are available to secure a hem without stitches. Follow manufacturer's instructions. Be sure to test fusible agent on a scrap of fabric before making hem.

These special hem tips will add more interest to your hems and still help you retain the quality of the garment. They may be used on the most fashionable attire.

4. Hem and facing mitre: Use on skirts, dresses and jackets. *Clean-finish* as desired. Turn hem and facing to outside at corner; pin (A). Form *mitre* at corner using *mitre* method 2. *Stitch* hem and facing in place with one or two rows of stitching (B).

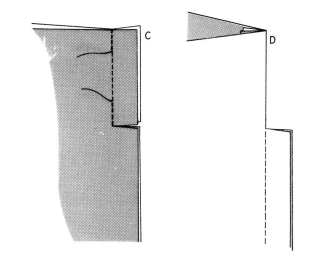

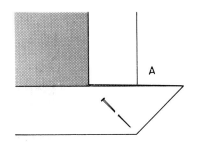

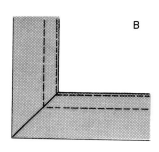

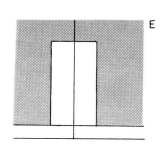

5. Band trim hem: Use durable trims that have the same cleaning requirements as the fabric. Allow 13 mm for the hem allowance. At a *seam*, make a 15 mm *clip* at least 13 mm above proposed *hemline* or 6 mm narrower than the trim. With wrong sides together, *stitch* seam to clip (C). On the inside, stitch remainder of seam (D). *Press* seam open above and below clip. Turn 13 mm hem to the outside; press (E). Pin trim over hem with one edge even with pressed edge; stitch both edges in place, turning in remaining raw end 13 mm and *lap* over first end. To *mitre* the corner of band trim, use *mitre* method 3. Stitch both edges of trim in place (F).

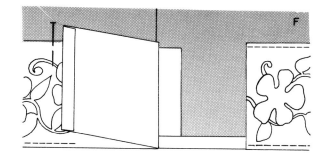

6. Ruffle trim hem: Select a single edge ruffle (type 1) or a ruffle with a heading (see *Ruffles* type 2) to finish a hem edge with a *ruffle*. Subtract the finished width of the ruffle from the garment length. For a single edge ruffle, use a 25 mm hem allowance. With right sides together, pin inner row of gathering stitches on *hemline*; *stitch* just inside this row of stitches. Turn hem down over raw edges of ruffle. Turn in raw edge 6 mm and cover raw edge of ruffle; stitch through all thicknesses, keeping garment free (A).

For a ruffle with a heading, use a 6–13 mm hem allowance depending on the space between the *gathering-stitches*. Turn hem allowance to the outside; press. Pin and stitch ruffle in place so pressed edge will cover the lower row of gathering threads (B).

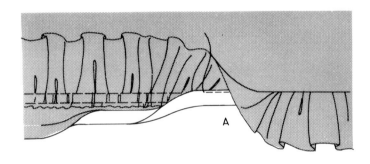

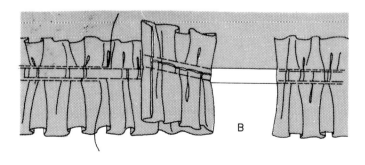

Hemline

The actual spot or line where the hem is folded to the inside. Mark fold accurately when using to apply trim.

Hook and eye

A classic closure that will withstand strain and not pop open. There are some new hooks available including: Velcro® strips specifically designed for waistbands; a large hook with an adjustable band of eyes; a large, flat hook and eye suitable for waistbands and no-sew hooks and eyes that are fastened with a hammer.

There is a simple trick that will make openings lie flatter when the classic hooks and eyes are used. After the circular ends are *sewn* in place slip needle under the fabric to the opposite end where the hook curves upward from the garment. Fasten this end securely with threads over the hook shank (A). When using a rounded eye, be sure to *sew* each side of the eye flat to the fabric after the circular ends are sewn in place (B).

Hook and eye tape fastener

See *Tape fasteners*, type 3.

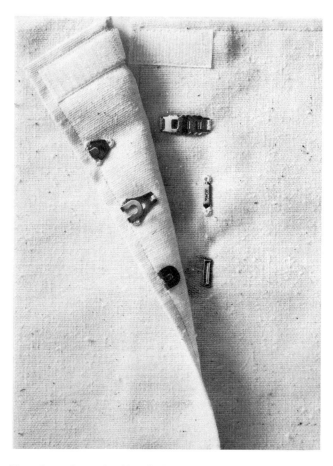

These fantastic new hooking devices are perfect for skirts, pants, and other garments that are used for sports and casual wear.

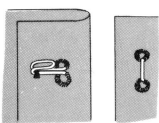
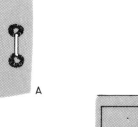
A

B

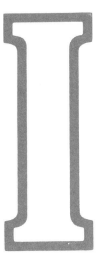

I

Insert (inserted)
A procedure whereby sleeves, bands, trim, and other fashion details are inserted in an opening or between two garment sections. A zipper may be inserted in an opening, a sleeve may be inserted in an armhole, or a band may be inserted in the front of a garment for an opening.

Interfacing
An additional layer of fabric placed between the outer garment layer and facing. Used to preserve shape and reinforce edges. Designers are again eliminating interfacings for the newer *unstructured* look. Select a weight of interfacing that won't overwhelm the *fashion fabric*.

Interlining (interline)
A layer of fabric designed for warmth that is used with the lining. To interline, cut same as lining. Place wrong side of lining over underlining with raw edges even; pin. Machine-baste 13 mm from the cut edges and handle as one layer of fabric throughout construction same as for *underlining*. Be sure to baste through centre of any darts or tucks.

Inward
A term used for a corner or curve that is shaped inward on an edge or seam of a garment. See *Seams* and *Bias binding*.

Iron-on
A general term used for fabric and interfacing which have been treated with a bonding agent. These fabrics are attached with the heat from the iron. See *Fusibles*.

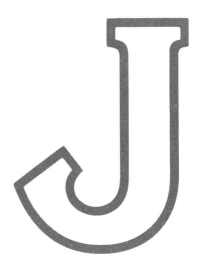

J

Jacket collar with lapels
See *Collars*, methods 4 and 5.

Jacket lining
See *Lining.*

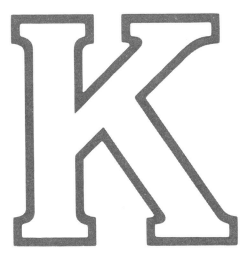

K

Kimono sleeves

Sleeve extensions of the garment that are at right angles to the body, somewhat like a "T". This type of sleeve creates folds at the underarm when worn and must be loose-fitting for comfort. Be sure to reinforce the underarm for durability. *Stitch* shoulder *seams*; finish neck and opening edges. Stitch underarm and side seam. After the seam has been stitched, *clip* curve and press seam open (A). Use a strip of commercial bias tape pressed open. Cut strip in half lengthwise or use a narrow bias self-fabric strip. Centre over curved seam; pin. Stitch 3 mm each side of the seam through all thicknesses (B). Finish the sleeve edge with one of the quick and easy hems or other finishes shown throughout the book.

Knits

A general term for the knitted fabric used by the home-sewer. Because of their easy care properties, knits are favourites. Select the right type for your pattern. Read the entire pattern envelope carefully for tips. See section, A Fast Start.

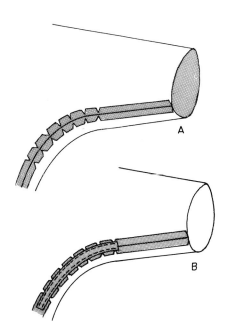

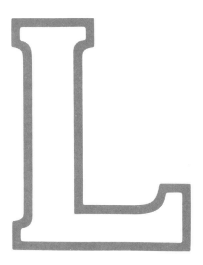

L

Lap

A term used when one edge extends over another. An opening or placket is lapped; so are ends of trim.

Lapel

The portion of a garment that folds away from the front centre line near a neck edge. Lapels are usually made with a collar as in a blazer. See *Collars*, methods 4 and 5.

Lapped seam

A procedure used for interfacing usually at the centre back seam of an undercollar. Simply *lap* one edge over the other, matching *seamlines*. Zigzag the layers together along the seamline.

Leather

See section, A Fast Start.

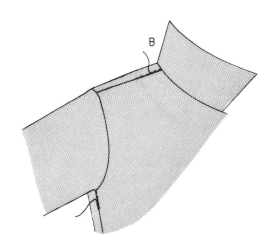

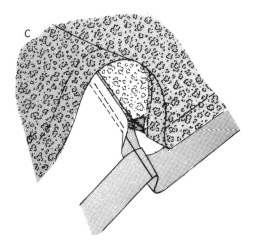

Lining

A layer of fabric or a number of fabric sections stitched together to cover the inside of a garment, concealing the seam allowances. The pattern instructions are quite easy to follow, but they may be time-consuming.

1. Easy machine method: Make garment but do not *anchor* facings. Then construct lining including the sleeves, making all pleats or darts. If sleeves are to be *sewn* in by hand, set them in on the flat as shown for *Set-in-sleeves*. Make *hem* in lining by machine. Turn facing to outside; pin lining to facing matching symbols and seams. Stitch lining to facing, keeping garment free (A). Press seam allowances toward lining. Turn lining to inside, slipping sleeves into the garment's sleeves.

Match shoulder and side seams; pin at the shoulder seam, stitch in seam groove through all thicknesses, the width of the facing, back-stitching at both ends. At the underarm stitch garment and lining together for about 38 mm in the same manner (B). At the side seam near the hem edge, turn back lining and pin the garment and side seam allowances together, keeping garment free. Stitch seam allowances together for about 50 mm (C).

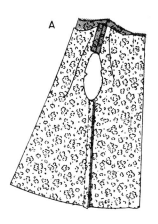

2. Lining when pattern does not give lining pieces or instructions: Some *unstructured* garments do not need a lining, however, your fabric may be scratchy and you may wish to cover it. To cut a lining, use the front, back, and sleeve pieces only. If front has an extended facing, cut lining 13 mm beyond the foldline. Add a 50 mm *pleat* (25 mm on the fold) at the centre back. Cut front and back to hemline. For a sleeve with a *cuff*, make lining 25 mm longer; with a *hem*, cut to *hemline*. *Stitch* front to back and stitch pleat for 50 mm at neck, waist and hem edge (A). Pin lining to garment wrong sides together over interfacing. Finish front neck and hem edges (B).

Stitch seam in sleeve lining. Slip over garment sleeve wrong sides together. Make *ease-threads* through both layers. For a cuff, keep lower edges of lining and sleeve even, forming a 13 mm pleat for wearing ease. For a hem make the same 13 mm pleat too (C). Insert sleeve as directed with pattern. Trim seam allowance to 6 mm and bind armhole with commercial double-fold bias tape or self-fabric *bias binding* (D).

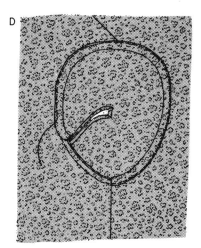

Loop

A folded and stitched fabric strip or a strip of trim that forms an opening at a garment edge through which a button is passed or serves to hold a belt in place. Everything is possible when sewing your own clothing: design your own opening with loops or *insert* a loop in a *seam* to hold a belt in place.

To modify a centre opening for loops: Cut out garment as instructed with pattern. For the right front (both garment and facing) turn back these pattern pieces 15 mm beyond the centre front marking. Re-pin pattern pieces to the right front **only** and cut away excess fabric.

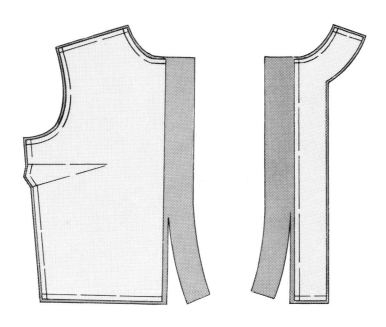

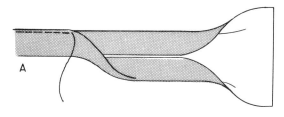

A

1. Fabric loops: Cut a *bias* strip four times the desired width and long enough to make as many loops as needed. Turn in long edges to meet at centre of strip; *press*. Bring folded edges together and press again. *Edge-stitch* folds together (A). Turn back 15 mm seam allowance on the right front. Pin strips to the folded edge at buttonhole markings. Form a loop large enough for button to pass through. The shape of the loop will vary according to the shape of the button. Round, dome buttons will need a longer, closer spaced loop (B). Flat buttons will need a short, spread loop (C).

When loops are positioned satisfactorily, *machine-baste* loops in place along centre front seamline. Complete garment as usual, catching loops in front opening seam. Sew buttons in place high enough so that the lower edges will hang even when garment is worn (D).

2. Narrow trim loops: Trim may be substituted for the fabric loops as explained in type 1 above. To use a loop as a decorative feature for casual garments, shape loops as directed in steps C and D above, over the *seamline*. *Stitch* in place along seamline and 6 mm from raw edge (A). Complete opening by turning in edge along seamline; press. Turn in raw edge 6 mm and stitch, forming a narrow hem (B). Sew buttons in place so their lower edges will hang even when garment is worn.

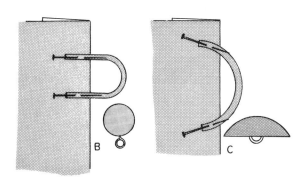

B

C

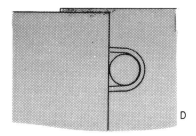

D

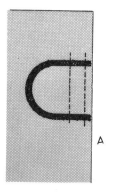

A

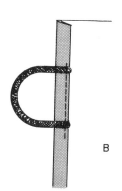

B

3. Belt carrier: Cut straight grain strips and make fabric loops as in method 1. Place strip over one section at the side seam with the ends above and below where the belt will be worn; *baste* (A) Catch loop in side seam, *back-stitching* over each end of the loop (B). *Insert* belt (C).

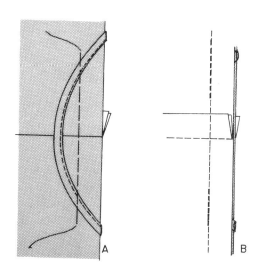

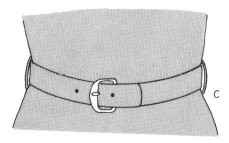

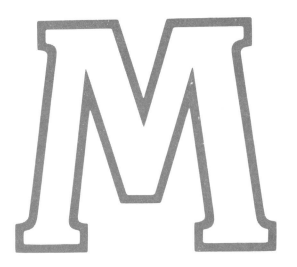

M

Machine-baste
A quick and easy way to hold garment sections together temporarily. Use the longest stitch possible for your machine. Loosen the top tension slightly so the threads can be removed easily.

Mark (marking)
The act of transferring pattern symbols and markings to fabric for speedier sewing. There are many classic ways to mark: dressmaker's carbon paper and tracing wheel is probably the most accurate way to mark, but it cannot be used on all fabrics. Be sure to test carbon paper on a fabric scrap before marking garment. Tailors' tacks may be used to mark any fabric except leather or vinyl.

These following methods are quick and easy for the experienced sewer:

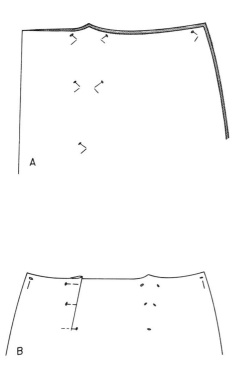

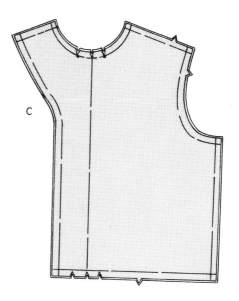

1. Pins: Insert pins straight through pattern and both layers of fabric to the other side. Remove pattern carefully forcing pin heads through tissue. Turn to underside, push pins into same point where first set of pins emerge. Separate layers, remove pattern and anchor pins securely (A). Pin all darts ready for stitching at this time (B).

2. Clips: Make scant 6 mm clips at markings in seam allowances (C). Do not clip when using flat-felled or French seams or if fitting may be required.

Matching plaids, stripes, and prints

A procedure that often will prevent good needle-workers from selecting a fabric that they really like. . . . Select a simple garment such as a bias or A-line skirt for your first project. Look carefully at the cutting layout and purchase an extra *design repeat* for each piece (or pieces) that takes over half the fabric width.

Work on a large flat surface, with the right side of the fabric facing you. For any piece to be placed on the fold or a centre seam, be sure to place the fold marking or seamline over the centre of the plaid or the centre of a predominant strip or print motif. Lay out the pattern pieces on the open fabric (don't pin) as shown on the cutting guide to get a general idea of the fabric design and where it will fall on each piece. Now cut out each piece: For a four-gored skirt cut out the right front. With the pattern piece still pinned, flip it over onto the fabric with the right front uppermost. You'll see how easy it is to match the design at all edges. Cut out the left front (A). You now have the front side seams so you can match the back perfectly. Turn back the right front side edges 15 mm; pin. Match with the right back side seamline (B).

When design is matched, cut out the back pattern piece same as you did the front (C), then cut out waistband. *Pin-baste* together at the seamline, placing pins as close as necessary to match all designs edges and complete skirt.

Men's wear

Denote men's clothing. While handsome tailored suits are an intrinsic part of every man's wardrobe, there are many procedures explained in this book that will help you make beautiful men's casual and sportswear, using the quick and easy shortcuts. See, *bands*, method 1; *casings*, methods 2, 4, 6, and 7; *collars*, methods 2, 3, 4, and 5; *cuffs*, methods 1, 2, 4, and 5; *flat-felled seam*; *hems*, methods, 1, 3, and 4; *lining*, methods 1 and 2; *mitre*, methods 1 and 2; *pants* creases; *pants*, hems, methods 1 and 2; *pockets*, methods 1, 2, and 3; *sleeves*, methods 1 and 2; *tape fasteners*, methods 1 and 2; *vents*; *waistbands*, methods 1, 2, and 3; *yokes*; and *zippers*, methods 1, 2, 3, and 4.

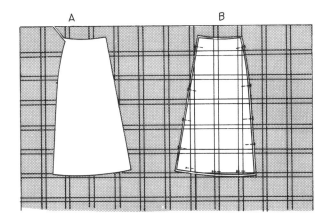

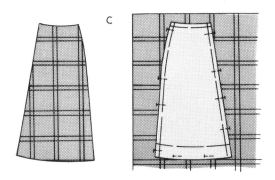

Metric measurements

The use of the metre as a standard measurement is being accepted everywhere and it is official Government policy that British weights and measures will gradually become entirely metricated. It is only a matter of time until the British use the metric system exclusively, as many other nations already do. Children at school are now taught in metric units only, but for those who were brought up on the old system of measurement, here is a conversion chart in which yards and inches are expressed to the nearest millimetre.

Inches	Millimetres(mm)	Centimetres(cm)
$\frac{1}{8}''$	3 mm	0·3 cm
$\frac{1}{4}''$	6 mm	0·6 cm
$\frac{3}{8}''$	10 mm	1·0 cm
$\frac{1}{2}''$	13 mm	1·3 cm
$\frac{5}{8}''$	15 mm	1·5 cm
$\frac{3}{4}''$	19 mm	1·9 cm
$\frac{7}{8}''$	22 mm	2·2 cm
1″	25 mm	2·5 cm
2″	51 mm	5·1 cm
3″	76 mm	7·6 cm
4″		10·2 cm
5″		12·7 cm
6″		15·2 cm
7″		17·8 cm
8″		20·3 cm
9″		22·9 cm
10″		25·4 cm
11″		27·9 cm
12″		30·5 cm

Yards	Centimetres(cm)	Metres(m)
$\frac{1}{8}$	11·3 cm	
$\frac{1}{4}$	22·6 cm	
$\frac{3}{8}$	34·1 cm	
$\frac{1}{2}$	45·7 cm	
$\frac{5}{8}$	57·0 cm	
$\frac{3}{4}$	68·5 cm	
$\frac{7}{8}$	79·9 cm	
1	91·3 cm	
$1\frac{1}{8}$		1·03 m
2		1·85 m
3		2·75 m
4		3·70 m
5		4·60 m

Mitre

Diagonal fold(s) made at a corner so seam allowances, *hems*, *facings*, and *trims* will form right angles. Mitres may be pressed or stitched into place.

1. To mitre seam allowances: Turn corner at a 45° angle where the seamlines intersect; *press* (A). Turn up edges along seamline, forming mitre; press (B).

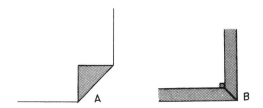

2. To mitre hems and facings: Turn garment edges to outside at corner. Grasp edges where they meet and pull out excess fabric forming a crease first on the facing and then on the hem (C). Match creases and *stitch* along mark keeping garment free (D). Trim to 6 mm and press *seam* open, being careful not to form creases in hem and facing folds (E). Turn to inside; press.

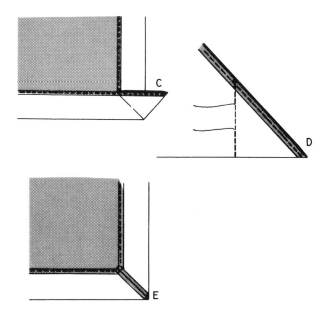

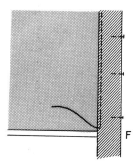

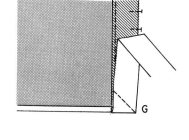

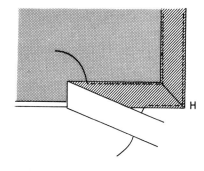

3. To mitre band trims: First mitre seam or *hem* allowance at corner following steps A and B. With trim pinned even with pressed edge, stitch inner edge to opposite side; break stitches (F). Turn trim back over itself with fold even with pressed edge. Fold trim again, forming mitre and crease. Stitch along crease (G). Pin trim in finished position. Stitch remainder of inner edge, then stitch entire outer edge together (H).

Motif

A dominant figure or design printed or woven in a fabric such as a predominant flower or circle.

N

Nap (napped)

Soft surface of fabric with fibres that lie smoothly in one direction. Napped fabrics must be cut in such a manner that all garment pieces have the napped surface all going in the same direction on the body. Corduroys, and velvets, are the easy napped fabrics to identify. Many knits, satins, and woollens that reflect light must be cut like a napped fabric. One-way prints must also be cut out like *napped fabrics*. To test fabric, hold it on your body in a well-lighted room. Look down over it, then reverse the fabric so it's hanging in the opposite direction. If it is dull one way and bright the other, you have a napped fabric.

Neatening

See Clean-Finish.

Neck and armhole facing combination

The instructions given in commercial patterns are quite adequate. This is one time that seams are stitched and then the zipper applied after the facing is stitched in place. To prevent facings from showing on the outside of the garment pin a narrow tuck across the shoulder seams. Pin facing to garment, matching shoulder seams with back or front opening edges even (facing edges will extend beyond the garment edges across the shoulder area). *Stitch* neck and armhole 15 mm from the facing edges. Remove pin tucks; *trim* and *clip* seam allowances. Turn right side out by pulling each back or front section through the opening between the facing and garment at the shoulder seams. Complete opening and then stitch side seams same as for *Armhole facing*, method 2 step C.

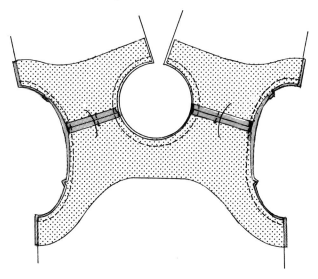

Neck facings

Insert zipper if needed in the garment back or front sections. Then *stitch* the shoulder seams only so you can work on a flat surface.

1. Shaped: *Stitch* facing to garment as instructed in the pattern's sewing guide. Now comes the crucial part: For light- and medium-weight fabrics, *trim* seam allowances to within 6 mm of stitching, trimming interfacing close to stitching. *Clip* curve (A). For heavy fabrics, *trim* and *grade* seam allowances and *clip* curve (B). For all fabrics press seam toward facing and *understitch*. The understitching is the most important step of the whole procedure; it helps hold the facing on the inside and will automatically *favour* the garment as it is turned in and *pressed*. Pin facing to garment matching shoulder seams and *tack*. To finish facing ends, turn in raw edges to clear zipper teeth. *Stitch* ends in place along zipper stitches (C). Fasten with a *hook and eye*.

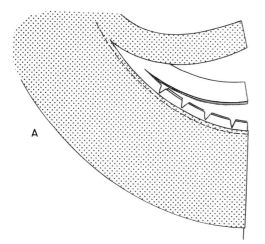

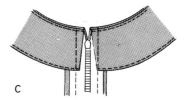

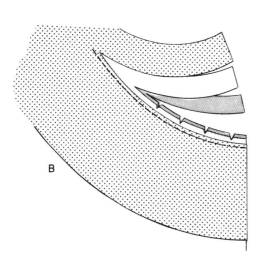

2. Commercial single-fold bias tape: *Press* open one fold, then shape the tape to fit the neck edge by stretching the remaining folded edge and shrinking the raw edge (D). Pin to garment, placing tape crease 15 mm from cut edge. *Stitch* along crease. *Trim* excess seam allowance even with tape, *clipping* curve (E). Turn tape to inside along seam, *favouring* garment edge; press. Pin in place. Turn in ends to clear zipper tape; pin. *Edge-stitch* folded edge to garment; stitch along zipper stitching and edge-stitch along the neck edge, ending over beginning stitches (F). For special fabrics or garments, *sew* folded edge in place with *slip-stitch*, method 1.

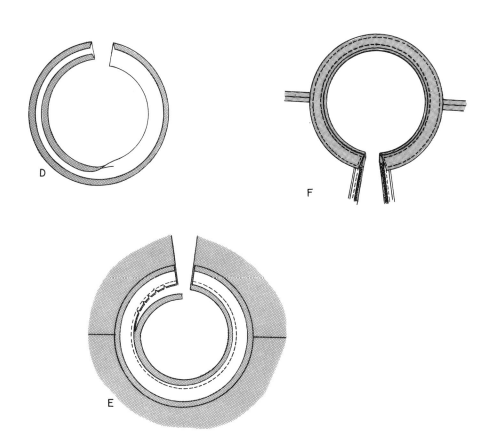

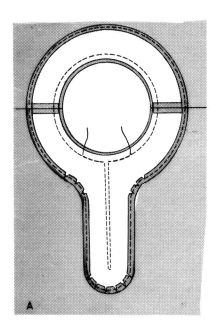

A

3. With a slit opening: When a garment goes easily over your body and you want to eliminate the zipper, but you need a larger opening for your head, simply modify the front facing and stitch the back seam shut. Cut the back facing on the fold at the seamline. Add a 15 cm extension to the front facing making it 10 cm wide, shaping ends and sides as shown. Make a line 16·5 cm deep along the centre of facing. *Stitch* facings together at shoulders. Stitch facing to neck edge; use 20 stitches to 25 mm, stitch 3 mm (the width of the narrowest toe on your presser foot) each side of the line, making a rounded point at the end, connecting stitches at neck edge (A). *Trim* neck edge same as for a shaped facing and slash along the line to the end of stitching for opening, *clipping* curved end. *Trim* corners (B). Turn facing to inside *favouring* garment edge; press. *Tack* at shoulder seams. *Edge-stitch* neck and slash opening edges (C). Stitch again 6 mm away, if desired.

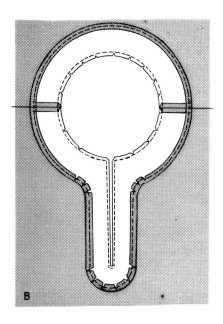

B

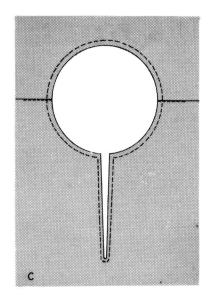

C

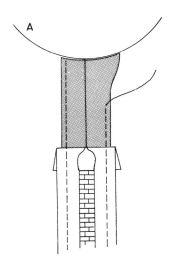

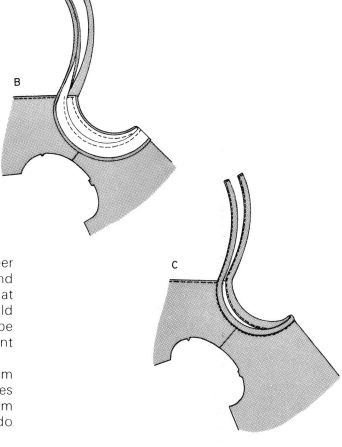

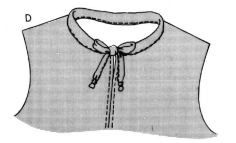

4. Bound with tie ends: A good finish for sheer and soft, lightweight fabrics. Prepare binding and neck edge as explained in *bias binding*, adding at least 30 cm for the ends. Commercial double-fold bias tape may be substituted or use wide bias tape and press in half with one edge extending a scant 3 mm. *Insert zipper* before binding.

For a glamorous opening, use a zipper 10–15 cm shorter than the opening. Turn in the raw edges above the zipper to meet the basted seam to form narrow *hems*; pin. *Stitch* hems in place as you do the zipper (A).

Remove basting. Stitch shoulders; add reinforcement stitches and trim neck edge. Divide shaped binding in half; pin at fold. Open binding, placing pin at centre front or back of neck edge with narrowest edge next to the garment. Pin to neck edge with raw edges even; stitch between narrow hems or zipper opening keeping tie ends free (B). Turn binding to inside over seam; pin, making sure remaining fold covers the stitches. Starting at one tie end, stitch folds together; continue along neck edge, stitching in the groove made where the binding joins the garment (make sure remaining edge of binding is caught in the stitches); stitch to the end of last tie end (C). Knot each end and tie into a bow (D).

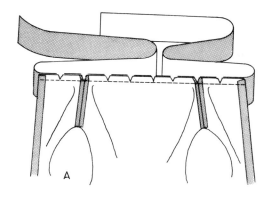

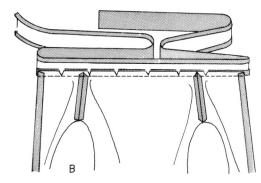

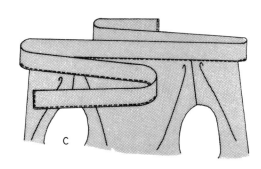

5. Straight strip neckband and ties: A great finish for jackets, robes, capes, sportswear and sleepwear that have openings that meet at the centre front. It works well in most fabric weights. *Reinforce* neck edge with a row of stitches and *clip* at even intervals. For a 25 mm wide band and ties, cut a 80 mm wide straight grain strip the length of the neck plus 45–60 cm. Divide strip in half; mark. Pin strip to garment with mark at centre back. *Stitch* to neck edge in 15 mm seam (A). Press seam toward strip and turn in remaining edge 15 mm; *press* (B). Fold strip in half, covering neck seam allowances; press and pin. *Edge-stitch* pressed edges together (C). Tie into a bow (D).

Neckline finishes

Any sewing procedure that is used to protect or decorate the neckline edge of a garment. See *collar, neck facings, bias bindings, tie closures.*

Needles

Whether used for hand- or machine-sewing, needles must be fine enough to slip through the fabric and still be easily threaded. Some knits created a problem of skipped stitches when *stitched* by machine. Ballpoint needles were introduced, but still the problem exists when sewing some doubleknit polyesters. Now Singer has a yellow needle that stitches these fabrics beautifully.

When stitching leather or fake leathers and suedes, use both hand- and machine needles specifically designed for leather. The hand-sewing needles are sometimes called "glovers" needles.

Non-woven

A growing list of fabrics that are made by pressure, heat, and chemicals. These fabrics do not fray or ravel and have no grain so garment pieces can be cut in any direction. Felt and interfacings are the most familiar non-woven fabrics with leather- and suede-looks becoming popular. One manufacturer has developed a suede-look that is better than real suede because it is washable.

Notch

1. As a matching point: small triangles printed in the seam allowances on commercial patterns, used to match up pattern pieces accurately. When cutting out your fabric, cut around each notch or set of notches (A).

2. As a *trimming* step: Small wedge shapes should be cut out of the seam allowances of *outward* curves to eliminate bulk and ridges when the garment is completed. To find out how much must be notched away, turn the seam allowances to the finished position. The ripples that form indicate the amount of excess fabric that needs to be removed. Pinch ripples together and trim away V-shaped wedges, being careful not to cut garment (B). Note: For sheer and lightweight fabrics pinking sheers are a good tool to trim away the excess seam allowance and cut out notches at the same time.

Also see *clip*, *grade*, and *trim*.

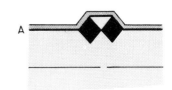

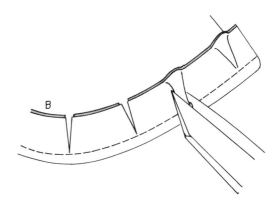

Notions

A term used by pattern companies on each pattern envelope to list the items such as thread, buttons, lace, zippers, etc., needed to complete a specific garment.

Nylon tape fastener

See *Tape fastener*, type 2.

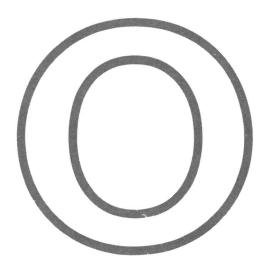

O

Open-work fabrics
See section, A Fast Start.

Openings
Areas in a garment that will open for easy removal
or wear.

Outward
A term used to describe convex corners and curves
on an edge or seam of a garment. See *Seams* and
Bias binding.

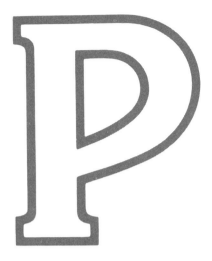

P

Pants

Men have always known the comfort and freedom of pants. Now, women consider them a necessary part of their wardrobe. When you find a pants pattern that fits well, protect it: purchase the non-woven, see-through fabric especially made for patterns or use tightly woven muslin and make a permanent pattern. Cut it out carefully using the tissue pattern. Transfer all markings with tracing wheel and carbon. Then make the marks more durable by tracing over them with a fine-point, felt-tip pen.

Pants creases

If your fabric doesn't hold the crease well, it's quite easy to stitch them in place. *Press* creases, making sure they hang straight when worn. Mark end of crease at fullest part of body. Pin each crease with the pin head away from the crease and the point about 3 mm away from the pressed edge. Starting at the mark, *stitch* about 1·5 mm from the crease, *back-stitching* at both ends.

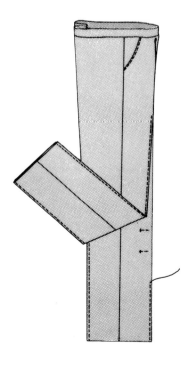

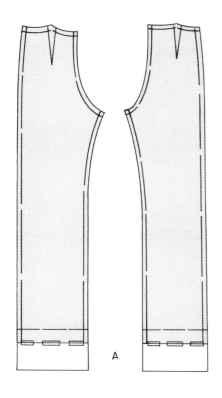

Pants hems

The basic hem procedures are used for pants hems too. See *Hem*. The narrow hem is especially good for shaped legs when the front is raised slightly to clear the shoe. There are two types of cuffs (turn-ups) that can be made quickly.

1. Classic cuff: To make a 31 mm wide cuff add 94 mm to each pattern piece below the *hemline* (A). When pants are stitched together, *clean-finish* raw hem edges. Turn up a 56 mm hem; *stitch* in place about 6 mm from inner edge. *Press* (B). Turn up folded edge 38 mm; press. Hold cuff in place by stitching in the groove through all thicknesses at side and inseams (C).

2. Simulated cuff: The cuff look and hem are made at the same time by machine. Add 13 mm to the lower edge of pants pattern, retaining normal hem allowance (A). When pants are stitched together, turn up hem allowance; *press* (B). Turn pressed edge down over the leg the width of the hem; pin. *Stitch* 6 mm from folds, catching raw hem edge in the stitching (C). Turn cuff down; press (D).

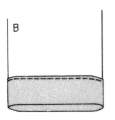

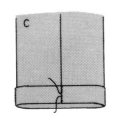

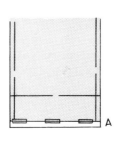

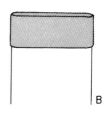

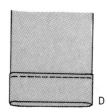

Pattern

For the home-sewer, this word has two meanings. It may be used to describe a fabric design such as floral, stripe, etc. It also may be used in reference to a paper pattern purchased with an instruction sheet that enables a person to make a garment, needlework, etc.

Pin-basting

The easiest way to hold fabric layers together for stitching. There are no fabrics that cannot be basted with pins when done properly.

1. Right-angle pin-basting (for fabrics that are not damaged by pin marks): A hinged presser foot is a "must" for this type. Place pins at right angles to the cut edge. Use as many pins as needed. For many seams three to five pins are sufficient—one at each end of the garment and the others distributed evenly (A). When matching designs such as plaids, pin at each intersecting line along the seamline (B).

2. Parallel pin-basting (for fabrics that may retain pin marks such as satin or leather): Pin in the seam allowance alongside the seamline (about 13 mm from the raw edges), placing the points away from you. As you stitch, remove the pins as the fabric feeds through the machine.

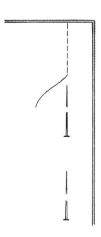

Pinking shears

Use pinking shears for procedures other than seam finishing. When used to trim enclosed seams made in sheer and lightweight fabrics, they will eliminate the need to clip or notch most *inward* or *outward* curved seams.

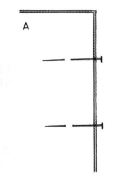

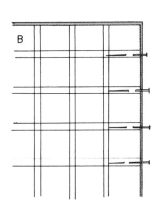

Pins

There are pins for every sewing need—from very fine pins for delicate fabrics to thicker ones for heavy fabrics. They come in several lengths, with coloured heads, and some have ball points to prevent fibre damage when they are inserted into the fabric.

Always purchase rust-proof pins. There may be an occasion when the pins may be left in the fabric for sometime and dampness will cause rust marks, ruining most fabrics. Pins are available in several thicknesses and lengths. Silk pins are made of brass and are 26–27 mm long; they are very thin with fine points. Use for fine, delicate and some sheer fabrics. Use Dressmakers pins in the 26 mm length and 0·65 mm gauge width (slightly thicker than silk pins) for general sewing. Larger Dressmakers pins, 37–38 mm long and 1·02 mm gauge, are designed for use with thick woollens. Plastic head pins 30 mm long and 0·65 mm gauge can be obtained for use on corduroy, other napped fabrics and woollens.

Pivot (pivoting)

A directive instruction. To pivot, *stitch* to corner. Stop with needle inserted in the fabric. Raise presser foot, turn or pivot fabric around needle so you can stitch the remaining side of the corner. Drop presser foot and complete stitching.

Plaids

A printed or woven fabric with crossbarred stripes. To match plaids when cutting out fabric, see *matching plaids, stripes, and prints.*

Pleats

Folds of fabric that add controlled fullness. Generally pleats are time-consuming because of all the marking required, but it is quite easy to change the look of your favourite A-line skirt pattern with the addition of a pleat at the centre front and centre back. Add 20–25 cm to the centre front fold marking and centre back seamline to make unpressed or stitched box pleats. Adjustment must be made in the yardage required for most sizes (A).

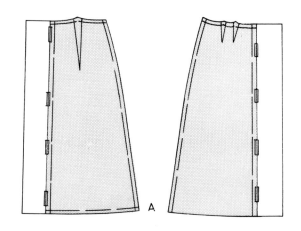

1. Stitched pleats: *Stitch* centre back seam below zipper marking. *Machine-baste* opening shut. Machine-baste the same distance allowed for pleat away from seam to within 15 cm of lower edge (B). Centre the seam over the inner row of machine-basting; *press* flat, pressing seam open and being careful not to press the pleat folds below the basting. Pin the pleat layers together securely around the basted zipper opening with basted lines matching. Apply *zipper* using method 1, stitching through all thicknesses (C).

Stitch along the centre front for about 17·5 cm; *backstitch* and break the stitching. Machine-baste below to within 15 cm of the lower edge (D). Centre pleat fabric over stitched and basted line and press (E). Top-stitch 6 mm from each side of pleat seam and across end at waist. Complete skirt as usual and remove pleat basting before hemming. Continue pleat creases to the hem edge.

2. Unpressed pleats: Mark fabric for pleats. After skirt is cut out, mark the original centre front and centre back and mark centre front fold with a pin. *Stitch* centre back seam and insert *zipper*. Crease below pins on the back, place creases even with zipper opening edges; pin (A). On the front, crease at pins; bring creases together at centre front; pin (B). Complete skirt.

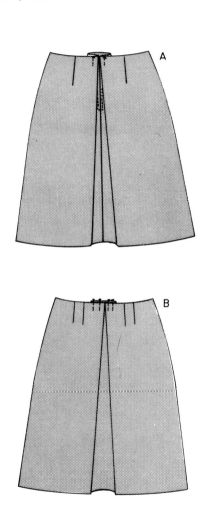

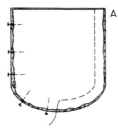

A

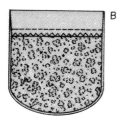

B

Pockets

Scraps of fabric are used to make a pouch-like appendage on a garment to hold small items. Pockets may be decorative as well as useful.

1. Patch: Use the pattern piece given or make your own shape, using a 38 mm hem allowance. Cut an extra section of self-fabric for each pocket to serve as lining when using light- to medium-weight fabric. Use a lightweight durable fabric as a lining for heavier pocket fabrics.

Pin the lining to the right side of the pocket extending the lining's edges 3 mm beyond those of the pocket, *easing* the pocket to fit. *Stitch* in a 19 mm seam, tapering the seam to 21 mm about 38 mm from the top edge (A). *Trim* seam; *notch* curves or *trim* corners. Turn right side out through top. *Press, favouring* pocket. Turn top down 38 mm or along foldline; press. *Clean-finish* raw edges, stitch hem in place (B).

Pin to garment at markings. *Edge-stitch* in place, forming wedge or a bar-tack with solid zigzag stitches at top, or topstitch again 6 mm away from edge-stitching (C).

C

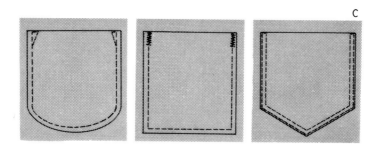

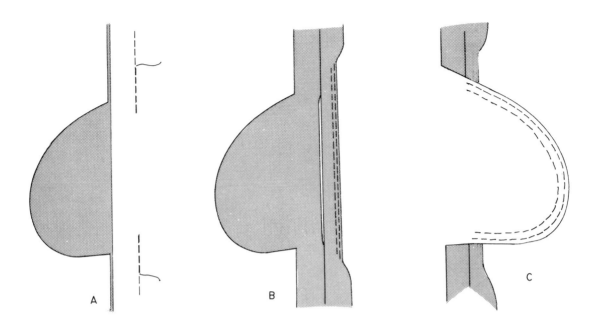

A   B   C

2. Pocket in a seam: Cut the pocket extension on the back garment piece only. *Stitch* side seam, back stitching at opening left for the pocket (A). Press seam open pressing the front seam allowance flat along the opening only. Turn in the raw edge 6 mm; *edge-stitch* in place. Stitch again 6 mm away (B). Turn pocket over opening; pin flat. Clip back seam allowance only at the top and bottom of pocket. Stitch 13 mm from raw pocket edges and again 6 mm away starting and ending at the seam (C). This makes a quick and easy durable pocket (D).

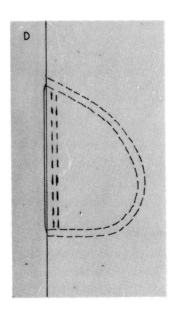

3. Slit buttonhole pockets: Mark position for pockets; usually about 7·5 cm below the waistline and about 5 cm from the side seams for teenagers and adults. Cut a rectangle of self-fabric 15 by 30 cm. Draw a line 12·5 cm from one end. Draw another line 6 mm above the line and another 6 mm below. Measure in 15 mm at each end and make rounded ends for the opening. Place strip over garment, right sides together, centring opening markings over the pocket position and pin. *Stitch* strip to garment along opening lines. Slash along the centre line and *clip* curved ends.

Turn strip to the inside through the opening; *press*. On the outside, *top-stitch* 6 mm from the opening edge.

On the inside fold pocket right sides together, stitch side and lower edges together, keeping the garment free. Zigzag the raw edges together for fabric such as denim that ravels easily.

A pocket on each side of the garment looks great.

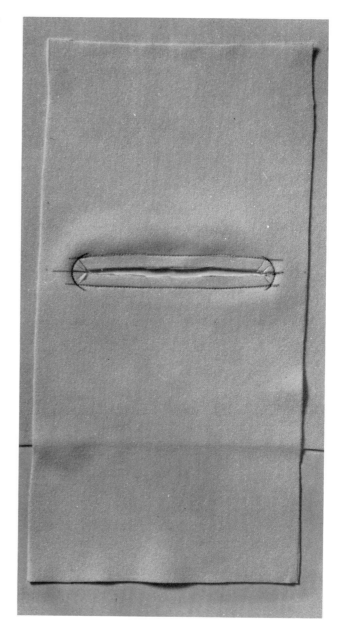

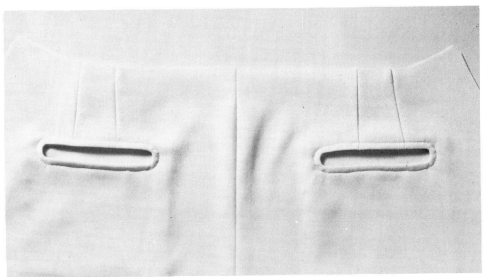

4. Slash pocket: Mark position for pockets 12·5–17·5 cm from the side seam just below the waist-line seam. Cut a rectangle of self-fabric 15 cm by 45 cm. On the wrong side, draw a line 15 cm long at the centre at one short end. Place marked end of the strip, right sides together, over the pocket marking on the garment; pin. *Stitch* strip to garment; using 20 stitches to 25 mm, stitching 3 mm (the width of the narrowest toe on your presser foot) each side of the line making a rounded point at the end of line. Slash to end of stitching, *clipping* curve.

Turn strip to inside; *press*. On the outside, *edge-stitch* opening edge and again 6 mm away. On the inside, turn strip up over the opening, making all raw edges even. Pin close to all raw edges. *Mach-ine-bast* edges in place.

On the outside of the garment, *top-stitch* close to pocket edges and again 6 mm away through all thicknesses along side and lower edges rounding the corners.

Pocket edges are held in place with the top-stitching.

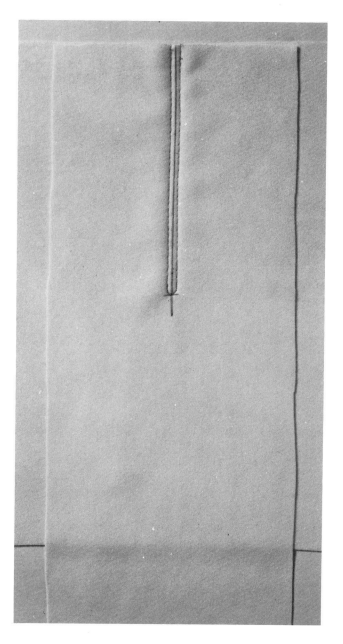

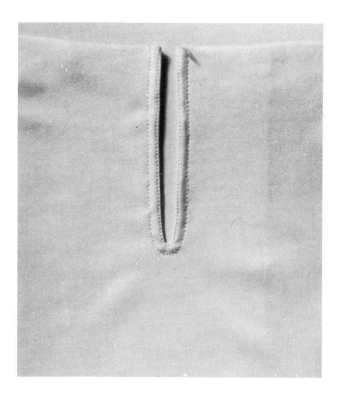

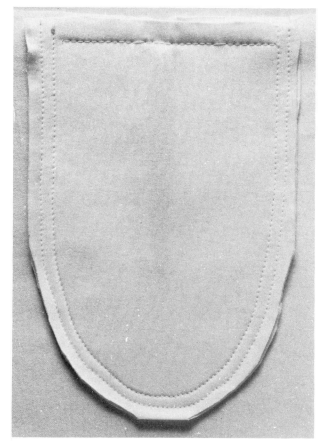

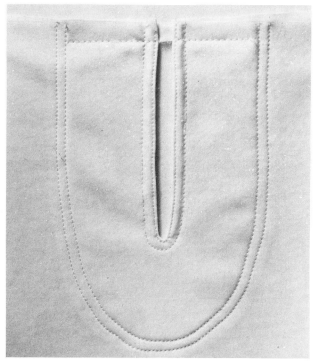

Press

Lift up iron and set down on an area to be pressed. Do not slide iron over the fabric. Pressing is one of the most important procedures necessary to speed up sewing. Set up ironing board and iron near the sewing machine and use it often. A metal ruler with a slide to mark the measurements is a great helpmate, too.

Certain fabrics lend themselves to finger-pressing (press seams open with fingers, pulling a thumbnail or blunt object along the seam), but most, especially knits, require the use of the iron.

Do not overpress or the fabric may become shiny and the seam allowances may cause ridges on the outside of the garment.

There are many pressing gadgets available to aid in the speed-up, but you may use substitutes that work just as well.

Using the correct pressing equipment will speed up your sewing projects. Starting on the left, look at the following pressing aids on the ironing board: press mitt, point turner, needleboard, seam roll, tailor's ham, point presses with pounding block, sleeve board, and iron.

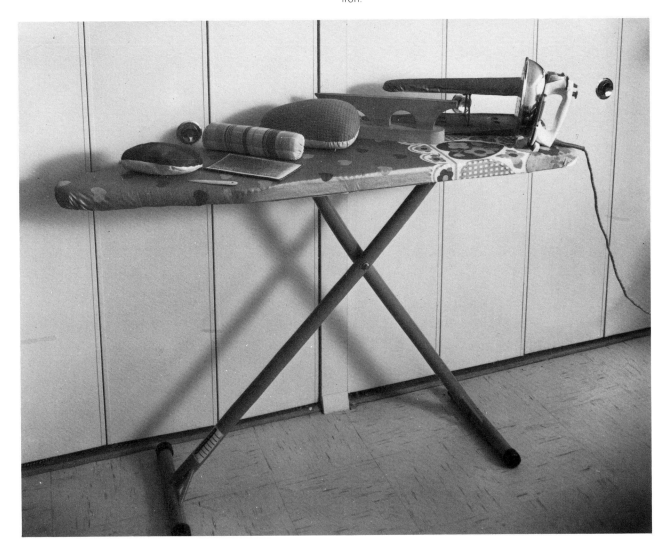

1. Seam roll: Used to prevent imprint of seam allowances on the right side of the fabric. Substitute 10 cm wide doubled strips cut from a brown paper bag without printing (A).

2. Sleeve board: Use to press seams open so unwanted creases are not pressed in. Substitute several tightly rolled magazines covered with turkish towel pinned securely with safety pins. Insert in the sleeve or pants leg to press the seams open (B). Or place sleeve or pants leg over the edge of the ironing board; pressing the seam open being careful not to press creases in the portion lying on the board. Note: Place strips of brown paper between the fabric and seam allowances to prevent a seam imprint.

3. Tailor's ham: Use to form contours such as darts, curved seams, and collars. Substitute a small, hard pillow or a tightly balled turkish towel pinned securely with safety pins (C).

4. Point presser: Use to press *enclosed* seams open before the garment section is turned right side out in order to achieve a sharper, smoother edge. Substitute a wooden dowel with a point, or cut several layers of cardboard the shape of the pattern piece (D).

5. Needleboard: Use to press corduroy and other pile fabrics. Substitute a thick turkish towel or a scrap of self-fabric (E).

6. Pressing cloth: Use to prevent shine or iron marks. Many inexpensive pressing cloths are available, including a see-through one. When pressing pile fabrics, use a scrap of self-fabric. A dampened turkish towel makes a good press cloth for heavier fabrics. Press appliqué, embroidery, and other raised surfaces face down on a turkish towel.

Press Fasteners
See Snaps.

Print
Fabric with designs printed on the surface. Prints may be an all-over design that does not need matching, a one-way design that must be cut like a *napped* fabric, or a large design that must be matched. Also see *design repeats*.

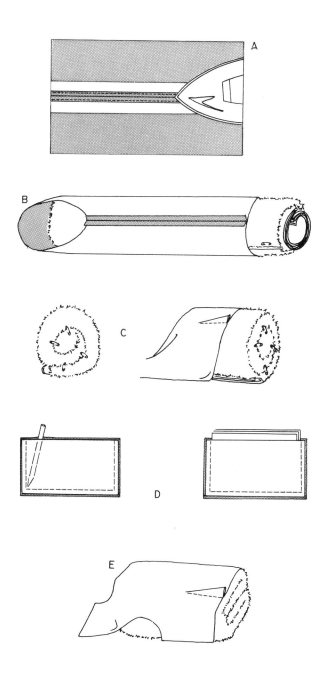

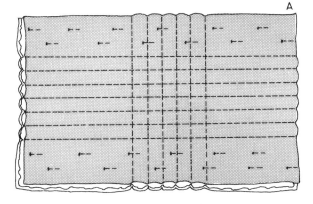

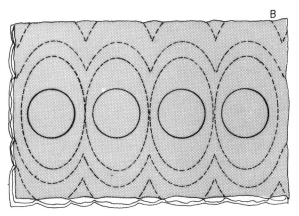

Q

Quilt (quilting)
Three layers of fabric stitched together, forming
one puffy layer of material. Use one layer of *fashion
fabric*, one layer of polyester batting, and a layer of
lightweight fabric for a *backing*. Use fabric scraps
to make quilted yokes, collars, and pockets for a
garment or be really ambitious and quilt fabric to
make a vest or other easy-to-make garments.

To prepare material for quilting, pin all layers
together starting at the centre, using long pins or
safety pins. Pin at about 15 cm intervals. Use matching or contrasting thread, a quilting foot and 8 to
10 stitches to 25 mm, and slightly less pressure on
the presser foot. Stitch squares, lines or diamonds,
marking the first row in the centre of the *fashion
fabric* before pinning it to the other layers. Then
make the remainder of the rows using the space
guide on the quilting foot to keep the spaces even
(A), or, stitch around a design motif (B).

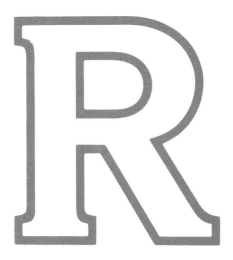

R

Raglan sleeves

These sleeves are easy to make and easy to wear. The sleeve section extends to the neck edge and usually has a dart along the shoulder for shaping. *Stitch* dart or seam in sleeve. Pin sleeve to garment front and back (do not stitch side seams). To reinforce, place a narrow strip of self-fabric or seam binding along each curve; pin. Stitch seams (A). *Clip* curves, being careful not to cut reinforcement strip. *Press* seams open. Stitch underarm and side seam; press open (B). Finish the sleeve edge with one of the quick and easy *hems*, *cuffs*, or other finishes shown throughout this book.

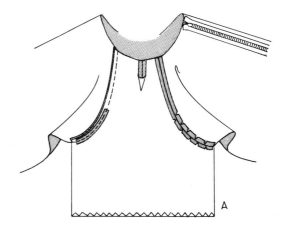

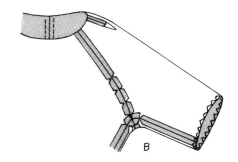

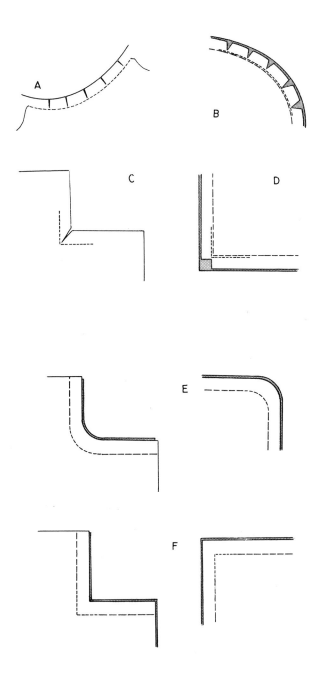

Reinforcing stitches

This type of stitching is used two ways to speed up sewing and make seams more durable.

1. To reinforce an *inward* (concave) corner or curve: This will release the seam allowance in order to stitch it to an opposite corner or curve. Use 20 stitches to 25 mm and stitch alongside the seam-line in the seam allowance (a scant 15 mm). For the inward curve, add the reinforcement stitches; *clip* to stitching at even intervals (A). Pin to opposite curve, spreading clips. *Stitch* seam alongside the reinforcement stitches on the garment side (B). For the inward corner, add reinforcement stitches; clip diagonally to corner (C). Pin to opposite corner spreading clips. Stitch seam alongside the reinforcement stitches on the garment (D).

2. To make curves (E), corners (F), points (G), and scallops (H) more durable after they have been *trimmed* or clipped: *Stitch* seams with the regular stitch length to within 25 mm of the area to be reinforced; change stitches to 20 to the 25 mm and stitch area, continuing 25 mm beyond; change stitches back to the regular length and complete seam. Note. Take one stitch across corners and points when reinforcing for neater edges.

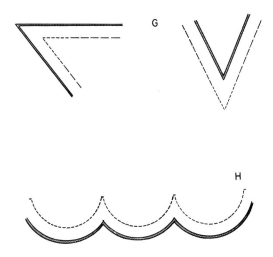

Ruffles

Those narrow strips of cloth or lace that are gathered, usually at one edge, and used as trim. There are several ways to make ruffles. They may be a single layer of fabric that requires only pressing. Cut ruffle $1\frac{1}{2}$ to 3 times the length of the edge where it will be stitched. Medium-weight fabric works best at $1\frac{1}{2}$ fullness; lightweight, at double fullness, and sheers at triple fullness.

Cut ruffle strips on straight *grain* or *bias*. When piecing strips, use a *clean-finish* on the seam allowances for a single thickness ruffle. Join ruffle in a continuous strip (when it will be added to hems or sleeves) or hem the ends. For a single thickness, make a continuous strip and then narrow hem (A) or narrow hem ends (B).

For a double thickness, make a continuous strip; press seams open. Then press, with wrong sides together and raw edges even (C) or stitch ends in a 6 mm seam and press same as continuous strip (D). Use heavy-duty or buttonhole twist thread on the bobbin and loosen tension slightly. For single ruffles to be joined in a seam, make *gathering-threads* from the right side of the ruffle. For all other ruffle types or applications, make gathering threads from the wrong side of the ruffle.

When applying ruffle, stitch on each side of the gathering threads so the heavy thread can be removed after the ruffle is stitched in place (E).

To distribute ruffle evenly over a long edge, divide ruffle into quarters; mark with pins. Break gathering threads at these points. Divide garment into quarters (more for long edges) and mark with pins. Pin strip to garment matching pins. Adjust gathers; distribute evenly. Add more pins. At outward corners, use fuller gathers so the ruffle won't curl; at inward corners, use less gathers.

Naturally, purchased ruffles are the easiest to use, but there may be times when a self-fabric ruffle is the "just right" trim needed. Use any sewing machine attachments you have. The narrower hemmer and the ruffler will save you time. Be sure to test fabric scraps before starting when using attachments. There are three types of ruffles:

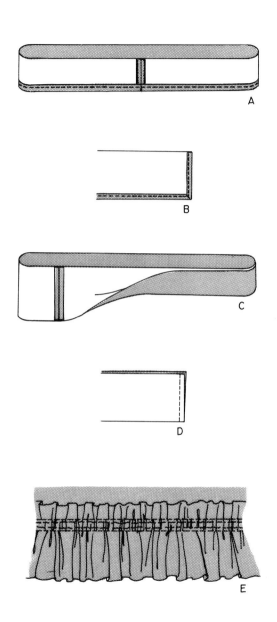

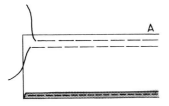

A

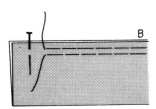

B

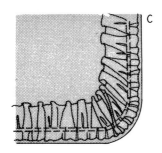

C

1. Single ruffles: One free ruffled edge that is caught in a seam on the gathered edge or held in place with trim. For a single thickness, cut strip the desired finished width plus 28 mm (15 mm seam allowance and 13 mm for narrow hem). Make ruffle strip; add *gathering-threads* (A). For a double thickness, cut strip twice the desired finished width plus 30 mm (two 15 mm seam allowances). Make ruffle strip; add gathering-threads (B).

To *insert* in a seam, pin and gather ruffle to fit; *machine-baste* to garment section along inner gathering-thread. *Press* seam allowance *only* with tip of iron (C). Pin remaining garment section over ruffle. Turn over and *stitch* from basted side using basting stitches as a guide (D). Finish seam allowance as required. *Trim* and *grade* a neck seam etc. Turn right sides out; *press* (E).

To apply a single ruffle with band trim, pin strip to garment and gather ruffle to fit; *machine-baste* to garment. *Press* seam allowance *only* with tip of iron and *trim* ruffle seam allowance if necessary to accommodate the band trim. Place band trim over seam allowance with lower edge covering stitches; *stitch* both edges of trim in place through all thickness (F). To use ruffles at a hem, see *Hem*, method 6.

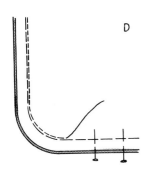

D

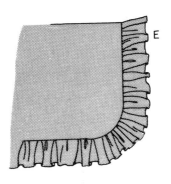

E

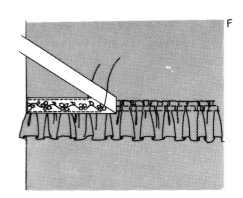

F

2. Ruffle with a heading: Two free ruffled edges that can be used just about anywhere on the garment or at the hem. For a single thickness, cut strip the desired finished width plus 25 mm (13 mm for each of two narrow hems). Make ruffle strip; add *gathering threads* 13–25 mm from one hemmed edge (A). For a double thickness, cut strip twice the desired finished width. Make ruffle strip; fold wrong sides together with cut edges meeting where the gathering-threads will fall; 13–25 mm from one pressed edge. Add gathering threads 3 mm from each raw edge through both thicknesses (B). Pin strip to garment and gather ruffle to fit. *Stitch* in place alongside both rows of gathering threads (C). To use ruffles at a hem, see *Hem* method 6.

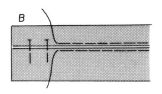

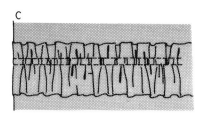

3. Double ruffle: Two free ruffled edges with each narrow ruffles measuring 19–38 mm wide. Apply anywhere that pleases you: along a hem edge, down the centre of a garment, or anywhere these frilly rows will enhance a garment. Double ruffles are made exactly like a ruffle with a heading with these exceptions: For a single thickness make gathering threads at the centre of the strip (A). For a double thickness, have cut edges meet at the centre (B). Pin strip to garment and gather ruffle to fit. Stitch in place alongside both rows of gathering threads (C).

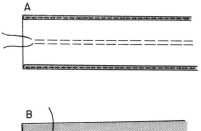

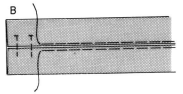

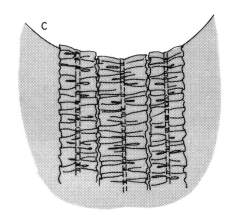

S

Seam

A line that is formed when two layers of fabric are joined together with a row of stitching. There are three types of seams used to construct a garment: *Structural seams* are used to stitch the shell, sleeves or legs of a garment together. These seams are usually stitched and then pressed open. *Enclosed seams* form finished edges on garments after they are *stitched*, *trimmed*, and the two outer layers are turned right sides out enclosing the raw seam allowances. *Lapped seams* may be used when you join interfacing or when the ends of *Bias binding* or trim are turned in and lapped to form a seam.

Set-in sleeve

This type of sleeve is joined to the garment in an oval shaped opening that encircles the arm at the edge of the shoulder where it joins the arm. Most pattern companies' sewing guides give you instructions to complete the sleeve units and then stitch into the garment's armholes. It is possible to stitch sleeves into the armhole on-the-flat. You may even eliminate the ease threads at the sleeve cap on some fabrics.

For stiff or bulky fabrics such as heavy double knits, corduroy, velveteen, vinyl, fake-suede and-leather, the extra fullness allowed in the sleeve cap for cupping over the seam cannot be *eased* in smoothly. If this happens, slide the fullness to the top at the shoulder marking and form a tuck. Pin tuck, and measure its depth (A). Remove sleeve and pull out ease threads. Make a fold in pattern above the notches one-half the tuck measurement (this fold across the pattern removes fullness at two spots along the seamline). Pin pattern to sleeve, matching notches: recut sleeve cap cutting a smooth line along the folds (B).

To set in sleeves on-the-flat, first stitch shoulder seams and finish neck and opening edges. Do as much on the sleeve as you can while they are flat. Make openings such as a continuous lap or other types given with the pattern, or see the opening treatments shown with *Cuffs*. For *Hems, clean-finish* the raw edge.

1. To set-in a sleeve without an *ease-thread*: pin sleeve to armhole, matching notches and symbols. Then distribute fullness evenly pinning about every 13 mm, with raw edges even. *Stitch* 15 mm from cut edges, when you come to the fullness, push fabric flat holding cut edges firmly with the right hand, stitching the sleeve cap while gently pulling horizontally with the left hand, stitching across the area to the next pin (A). With a little practice, you will need fewer pins and the procedure will go much faster.

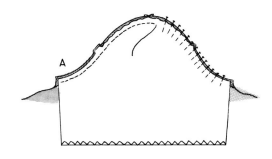

2. To set-in a sleeve with an *ease-thread*: Pin sleeve into armhole, matching notches and symbols. Adjust ease and distribute evenly. Add more pins as needed. With sleeve uppermost, stitch seam.

To reinforce the armhole seam for durability, stitch again 6 mm away; trim close to stitching between notches and underarm edges (B).

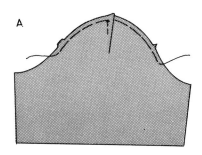

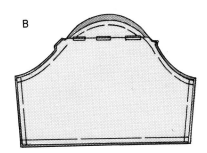

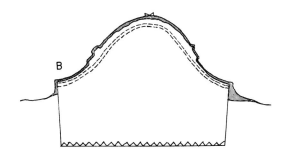

For loosely fitted garments, stitch sleeve and under arm in one continuous seam (C). For fitted garments, stitch the seam breaking stitches and *back-stitching* at the armhole seam (D). Press side and underarm seams open.

To finish sleeves, use any of the easy *hems* or an appropriate *cuff*.

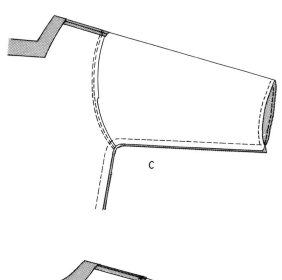

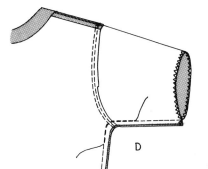

Sew (sewn)

Throughout this book the term sew will be an instruction directive for those procedures that are sewn by hand.

Sheer fabrics

See section, A Fast Start.

Shirring

Two or more rows of stitches used to hold gathered fabric in place below the seam. Shirring may be elasticized by using elastic thread on the bobbin (follow manufacturer's instructions) or it may be permanent. Allow double fullness for shirring and use soft, lightweight fabrics. Make rows as far apart as desired, using a quilting foot with a space gauge and the longest machine stitches, following same procedures used for *gathering*. Knot thread ends securely (A). If shirring is not anchored in the side seams, make narrow 3 mm wide *tucks* on each side over the knotted thread ends (B).

To make a shirred section, shirr a length of fabric. Trace outer pattern edges to gathered fabric. *Machine-baste* 6 mm from this edge and then add a row of *reinforcement* stitches near seamline (C). Cut away excess fabric.

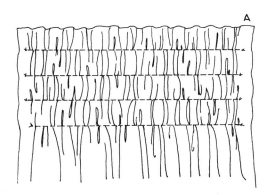

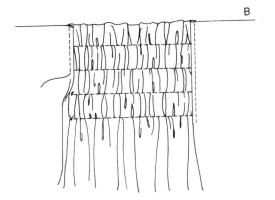

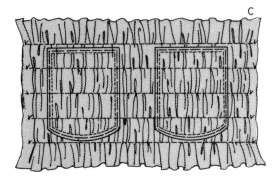

Slack

A term used by dressmakers when fabric lies or hangs too loose and limp. To remove the slack before stitching, carefully stretch the fabric while pressing it lightly with a steam iron. Some fabrics may shrink or retract slightly by simply pressing with a steam iron.

Sleeve finishes

Throughout this book, you will find many finishes that are suitable for sleeves. See *Hems*, all made by machine or finished with trims and *Ruffles*. See *Cuffs*, with easy openings and short-cuts for the classics.

Sleeves

There are three basic types of sleeves with many variations. The *kimono sleeve* is part of the garment. The *raglan sleeves* are separate pieces that form the sleeve and extend to the neckline over the shoulder. The *set-in sleeve* is a tube that is stitched into an oval-shaped hole in the garment.

Slipstitch

A durable, nearly invisible hand-sewing technique that is used to secure several types of edges.

1. Hemming stitch: Working right to left after anchoring thread, slip needle through folded edge at that spot, pick up a thread of the garment. Pull thread through and repeat the process making stitches about 6 mm apart (A).

2. For two folded edges: Work in same manner as for a hem. Slipping needle through fold closest to you while picking up a thread on the other fold (B).

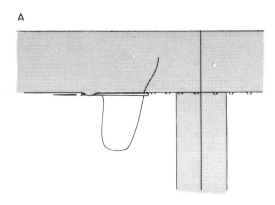

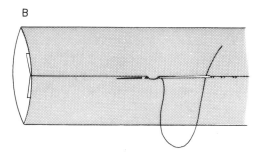

3. Applied sections (such as pockets, appliqués, and some trims): Work in same manner as for a hem slipping needle through fold of applied section, while picking up a thread on the garment. Curved edges may need stitches 3 mm apart (C).

4. Trims without folded edges: Work in same manner as for the hem, slipping needle through the garment while picking up a thread of the trim (D).

Smocking

A favourite embroidery technique where fabric is gathered with decorative stitches on soft, lightweight fabric. You may want to make smocking by machine as a speedy decorative touch. Make *gathering* rows as for *shirring*, step A, the desired spaces apart. Then cut out garment shape same as *shirring*, step B. Make rows of machine decorative stitches over *gathering-threads* (A), or use narrow bands of trim. Baby rickrack may be used to form diamonds over evenly spaced rows (B).

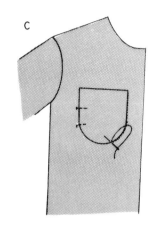

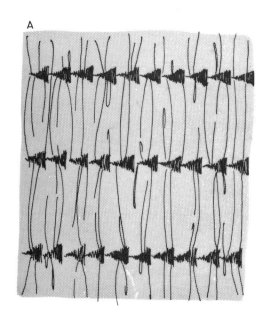

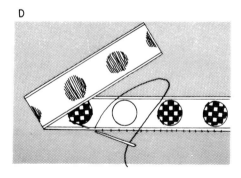

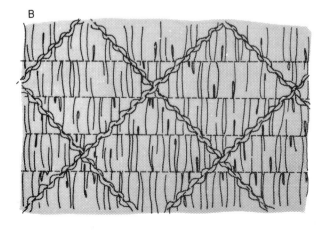

Slit buttonhole
See *Buttonholes*, method 1.

Snaps

A fastening device that closes by pressure. The classic metal snap comes in many sizes and is used on garment areas that do not receive strain from body movement. Two new snap closures that are being used everywhere are described below. Follow manufacturer's instructions for application procedures.

1. Velcro® circles and squares: one half of the snap has tiny nylon hooks and the other half has fluffy loops. The two layers are locked in place by pressure and will separate with a quick, sharp pull.

2. Hammer-on-snaps: these fasteners are anchored with a tool supplied by the manufacturer or a spool and a hammer. Buy the type recommended for the thickness of fabric you are using. Use them everywhere as they have both utilitarian and decorative styles.

Snap tape fastener

See *Tape fasteners*, type 1.

Soft fabrics

A general description of fabric that falls in fluid folds that hang straight down. This type of fabric should not be used for silhouettes that stand out away from the body. Batiste, some single knits, flannel, terry cloth, jersey and crepe are some of the classic soft fabrics.

Stable

A term used to describe firmly woven or knitted fabrics that do not stretch or pull out of shape when worn.

Stay-stitching

A directive term used by some pattern companies when two garment sections with opposite corners or curves must be stitched for a *structural seam*. To find out how to do this procedure, see *reinforcement stitching*, method 1.

Stitch (stitching)

Throughout this book the term stitch is an instruction directive for those procedures that are to be stitched together on the sewing machine.

Stripes

A printed or woven fabric with lengthwise, crosswise or diagonal stripes. To match stripes when cutting out fabric, see *matching plaids*, *stripes*, and *prints*.

Structured

A term used to denote garments that are made with *interfacing*, sometimes *underlining*, and that are usually *lined*.

T

Tab
A small strip of fabric attached at one end of a garment and buttoned or secured with another closure at the other end, or a loop attached to the garment to hold a belt in place.

Tab closure
See *Decorative closures*, method 1.

Tack
An instruction directive to anchor facings to the garment by machine or hand.

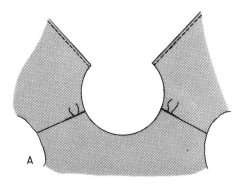

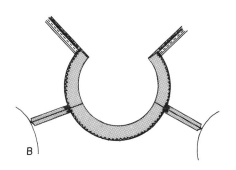

Tailoring

A term applied to *structured* garments made with classic lines and fashion details. Finely tailored garments are moulded into shape with hand-stitches and precise pressing. Today, even some of the most famous designers do not feature such garments. The few who do, use the finest fabrics available—*fashion fabric, underlining, interfacing,* and *linings*—and the craftsmen ply their trade with nimble fingers. The garments are quite expensive.

Tape fastener

Closing devices that are used in manufacturing clothes and are available to those who want a quick easy method. There are snaps and hooks and eyes attached to cotton tapes and a Velcro® tape that has one hooked and one lapped surface. These are practical fasteners for sportswear, sleepwear, and children's clothing.

1. Machine: Pin facing or cuff to garment matching seams. From the outside, tack in place by stitching along the groove made by the seam; *back-stitch* at both edges of facing or cuff (A).

2. Hand: Use to secure two garment layers together with a hand-sewn procedure. Most often used to anchor a facing to a garment. To tack, bring knotted thread up through seam allowance and facing, keeping outside of garment free. Make a stitch 6–13 mm long through these layers. Take 2 or 3 more stitches in the same place. Then insert needle under the facing to the remaining seam allowance and anchor to facing in same manner (B). Secure thread end by picking up one or two fabric threads with needle and take three tiny stitches in same place.

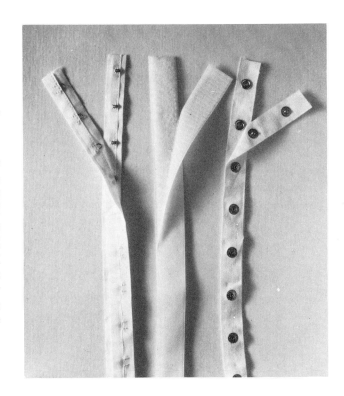

1. Snap tape: This type must be used with a lapped closing. It may be attached after the garment is completed or during construction.

To attach to a finished garment, place socket tape section over the centre front marking on the garment, placing one socket over the top buttonhole marking and end with a socket near the lower marking; pin. Turn in raw ends and *stitch* along the edges through all thicknesses, using zipper foot. Then pin ball tape section to the facing on the overlap, matching centre fronts and align the ball section with the sockets on the underlap. Turn in the raw ends and stitch along the edges through all thicknesses (A). To make a super closure, stitch a strip of decorative band trim over the stitches on the front.

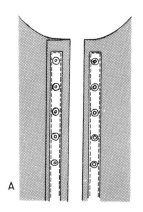

2. Velcro® tape: This fastener must be used with a lapped closing and may be attached to a completed garment or during construction following snap tape instructions above. Extend the tape 13 mm to 19 mm above the top buttonhole marking and the same distance below the lower buttonhole marking.

For an invisible application, attach during construction. Stitch the hook section to the garment front of the underlap and the loop section to the facing of the overlap (B).

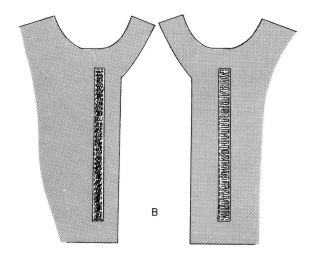

3. Hook-and-eye tape: May be attached to a completed garment or during construction. To attach to a finished edge, pin the hook tape section on the inside of the garment with the hooks along the edge, turning in both raw ends. Using a zipper foot, stitch along ends, long edge and around hooks. Now pin the eye tape section on the opposite edge with the eyes aligned with the hooks. Turn in raw ends and stitch the edges in place through all thicknesses (C).

Taper (tapering)
To make an edge or a line of stitching gradually become narrower into a point at one end.

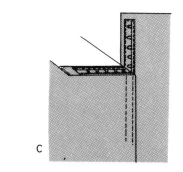

Tie closures

This type of fastener is most often used on a loosely fitted garment, but it can be used on any appropriate garment. If you have a dress zipper and it's too short, use *neckline finish*, method 4, that uses self-fabric *bias binding* with tie ends. To make a tie closure on the neck edge of a jacket or cape with centre edges meeting, see *neckline finish*, method 5, that uses a straight strip for neckband and tie ends.

1. To substitute tie closures for buttons and buttonholes: Cut straight grain or *bias* strips four times the desired finished width and as long as needed. Fold in half lengthwise with cut edges meeting; press. Fold at centre; press again. *Edge-stitch* the two folded edges together (A). Pin strips to garment to establish their position. Pin to garment with long ends turned away, *stitch* 6 mm from raw ends (B). Turn strip over stitched end and stitch 10 mm from fold (C). Tie to fasten (D).

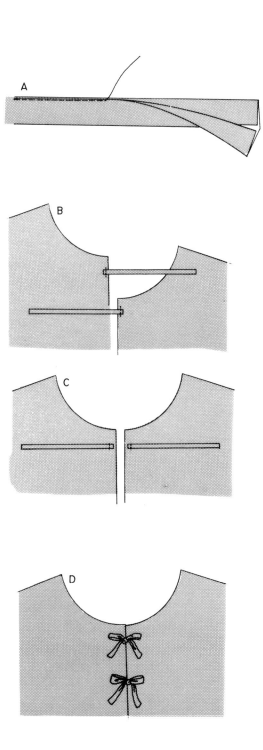

A denim wrap skirt is a favourite with women of all ages. The *tie closure*, method 1, was used to fasten the skirt at the waist.

Top-stitch (top-stitching)

To machine stitch on the outside of the garment. In some cases the stitching is done from the inside of the garment to hold hems and other edges in place. Other times it's meant to be strictly decorative and is made around the edges of a completed garment, or specific fashion details.

Trim (trimming)

A term that has two meanings that are both used for garment construction.

1. Any decorative band, motif, or appliqué used to decorate or finish a garment.

2. A technique used to make *enclosed* seams smooth when completed. To trim seam allowances, *grade* the layers to eliminate bulk. Trim any *interfacing* caught in the seam close to the stitching. Trim the top garment seam allowance to 3 mm and bottom one to 6 mm. For lightweight fabrics trim both layers to 6 mm. Pinking shears are great for this type of fabric (A). For a seam with a *collar* or *cuff* sandwiched between, grade the seam allowances starting with 3 mm and ending with one full seam allowance if necessary. Cut away any interfacing from the collar or cuff to the stitching (B). For a corner (C), or points (D), fold the seam allowances along the stitching. Any excess must be trimmed away so the edges will not overlap. For *outward* curves, trim seam allowances as instructed in steps A or B. Turn the seam allowances over the garment section along the stitching. The ripples will make lumps if not removed when turning right sides out. Trim away or *notch* out the ripples by creasing; cut away excess fabric (E). For inward curves, see *clipping*.

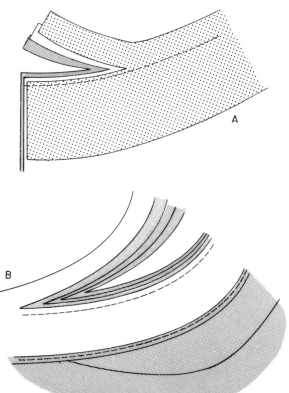

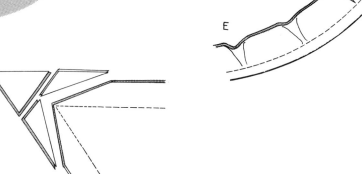

Trousers

See Pants.

Tuck

A fold made in a garment and held in place with stitches.

    1. Decorative tucks: Make in a fabric strip and then cut a garment section such as a yoke or pocket from it (A).

    2. Tucks used instead of darts: Stitch tucks from garment edge to a specific spot to add fullness over the body (B).

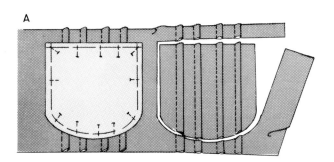

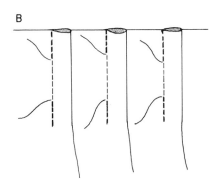

U

Underlining (underline)
A layer of fabric cut the same as the *fashion fabric*. Underlining is used for several reasons: to give support to the garment so it will hold its shape better; to hold all hems and other hand stitches on fine fabrics such as satin so they won't be seen on the outside, and to prevent shadows on loosely woven fabric so you cannot see through the garment.

Another good reason for underlining—all pattern markings can be made on the underlining with a tracing wheel and dressmaker's carbon paper. This prevents damage to delicate fabrics and is a quick and easy *marking* shortcut.

To underline, place underlining over wrong side of fashion fabric with the traced marking facing you. Pin down through the centre of each piece. Fold in half lengthwise along pins with fashion fabric uppermost over a Turkish towel. The underlining will extend slightly beyond the fashion fabric. (If this step is eliminated, the underlining will buckle under the outer fabric causing unsightly ridges.) Pin edges together as they fall

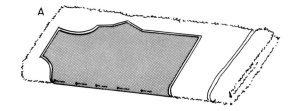

A

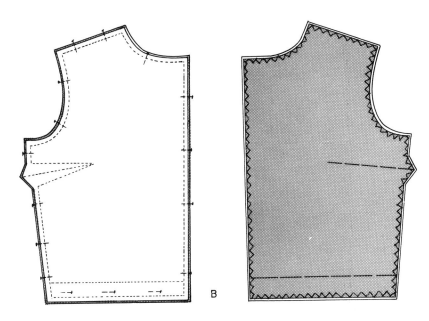

B

(A). *Machine-baste* 13 mm from fashion fabric edges or zigzag close to the raw edge. Trim away excess underlining if necessary. *Machine-baste* through the centre of darts or tucks and along proposed hemlines (B). Handle the two layers as one throughout construction.

Understitch (understitching)

A row of stitches placed on the inside of a garment that is used to prevent facing edges from rolling to the outside after the garment is completed. To understitch, *trim, grade,* and *clip* the seam allowances as necessary. Press seam allowances toward facing. Keep garment free and with the facing on top, stitch through all thicknesses (facing and seam allowances) close to the seam. Keep the facing flat as you stitch, spreading the clipped seam allowances of an inward curve so the facing will lie flat against the garment. A row of *edge-stitches* will serve the same purpose. Turn facing to inside, *favouring* garment, and press. Then edge-stitch.

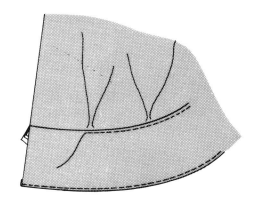

Unstructured

Garments that are made without *interfacing*, with exposed seams on the inside. They are often made with narrow hems instead of facings.

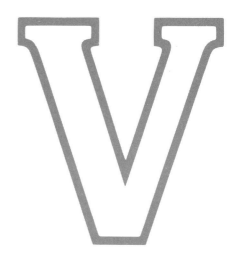

Velveteen
See section, A Fast Start.

Vent
Originally a slit in the back of a coat, now vents are used in many garments. To make a vent at the side seam of a blouse, dress, or jacket, end the seam 7·5–15 cm above the lower edge. Press the seam open, turning in vent edges 15 mm. Turn in raw edges at vent; pin. Prepare hem in lower edge of garment. Stitch hem in place continuing down one side of the vent, across the end and up the other side as you secure the hem. Note: Vents may have rounded corners.

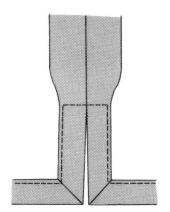

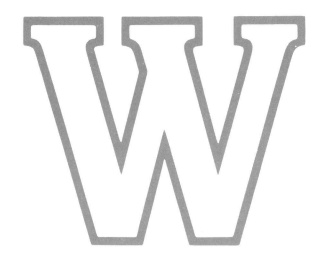

W

Waistband

The classic waistband is stitched to the outside of the garment and then *slip-stitched* on the inside. Some quick and easy shortcuts are in order.

1. Classic waistband: Prepare waistband and *stitch* to garment as directed on pattern's sewing guide. *Press* seam toward waistband. Turn in remaining raw edges 13 mm and pin to garment so it extends a scant 3 mm over the seam stitching; pin, catching only the garment layers so you don't make dimples on the outside. Turn garment wrong side out. Stitch in groove where the waistband is seamed to the garment, *back-stitching* at both ends (A).

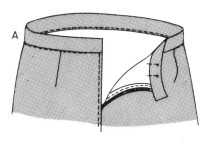

2. For heavy fabrics, place the unnotched edge 10 mm beyond the selvage or cut this edge to 6 mm after the waistband is made. Zigzag the raw edge. Stitch waistband to garment as instructed on the sewing guide. On the inside, place zigzagged edge 6 mm over stitching; pin and stitch as for step A (B).

For an easy to attach hook and eye, see *Hooks and eyes.*

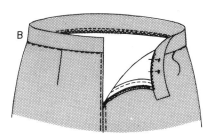

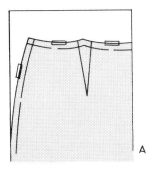

A

3. Elasticized waistband: Adapt pattern to accommodate casing. Make the waist circumference large enough to slip over the hips without distorting the style line. Add twice the width of the elastic plus 6 mm above the waist seamline for a casing. The darts are omitted (A). Cut elastic your waist measurement, less 10 cm; *Lap* ends 25 mm, stitch securely. Divide elastic in quarters by folding and mark folds with pins. Then divide each quarter in half. Divide garment edge into quarters and then eighths in the same manner; mark with pins (B). Place elastic on the inside of the garment, matching pins. Pin securely at matching points with edges even (C). Note: If garment front is wider than the back, allow a little more elastic at each side for the front.

Stretching elastic to fit fabric, zigzag the outer edge of elastic to garment (D). Turn edge to the inside, encasing the elastic. Stitch 3 mm from inner zigzagged edge stretching elastic to fit fabric as you stitch (E).

B

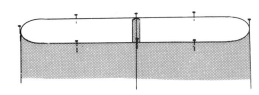

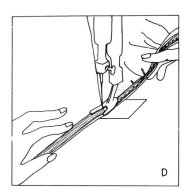

D

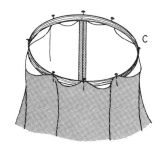

C

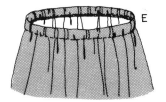

E

Take your favourite A-line skirt, make a front opening as explained
in A Fast Start, then add a casing that requires two rows of elastic
and you have designed a pattern for a high-fashioned garment.
Make it of double knit. Use 25 mm wide elastic, top-stitch front and
hem edges, and then use hammer-on snaps for an easy-to-wear
separate.

A

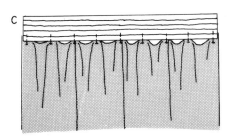

B

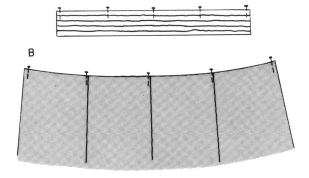

4. Decorative elastic waistband: Adapt pattern to accommodate the elastic. Make waist circumference large enough to slip over the hips without distorting the style line. The darts are omitted (A). Stitch all seams that form the waist but one; usually the centre back seam is not stitched. *Clean-finish* waistline seam allowances if necessary. Cut elastic your waist measurement plus 30 mm for seam allowances. (Check elastic to see if it is snug enough.) Mark a 15 mm seam allowance at each end with pins. Divide remaining length into quarters by folding; mark each fold with a pin. Then divide each quarter in half. Divide and mark garment in the same manner (B). Place wrong side of elastic over the right side of the garment, with the inner edge of elastic *lapped* 15 mm over the raw garment edge. Pin securely at matching points (C). Stretching elastic to fit fabric, stitch close to inner edge of elastic (D). Stitch seam, continuing across elastic, *back-stitch* at elastic edge (E). Press seam open. Stitch elastic flat, making sure ends do not show from the outside (F).

Waistline finishes
See *Casing*, *Drawstrings*, and *Waistband*.

Woven fabrics
See section, A Fast Start.

C

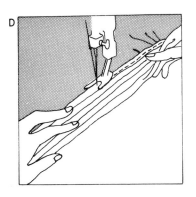

D

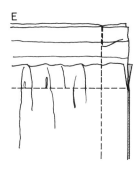

E

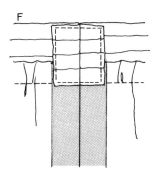

F

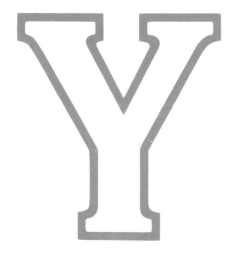

Y

Yoke
A small shaped garment section that is stitched to the major portion of a garment near the shoulders or hips. The yokes that are nearly straight lines do not cause any problems—it's the ones that require reinforced and clipped corners or curves that can drive you mad.

Yokes can be applied quite easily. Even this corduroy tunic was made entirely by machine without a clipped corner.

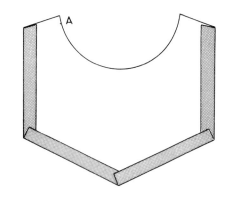

A

1. Set-in yoke with corners and/or points: Turn in the yoke edges 15 mm; pin, *mitring* corners and points. *Press* edge removing pins as you work (A). Place yoke over garment with raw edges even; pin. From the outside, *edge-stitch* yoke in place (B). Yoke may be *top-stitched* 6 mm from pressed edge and again 6 mm away instead of edge-stitching.

For a yoke that is cut double, clean-finish the raw edges of the facing, then complete the neck edge formed by the yoke and yoke facing. Turn yoke facing to inside. Pin facing over yoke seam, keeping outer layer smooth (C). From the outside, stitch close to the yoke, catching facing in stitching (D). *Top-stitch* as shown, if desired.

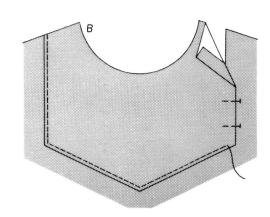

B

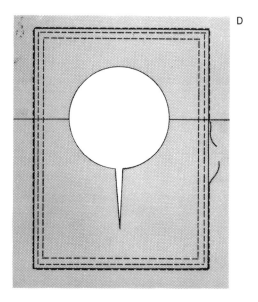

D

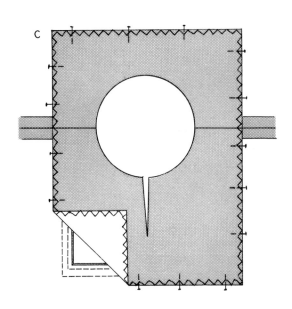

C

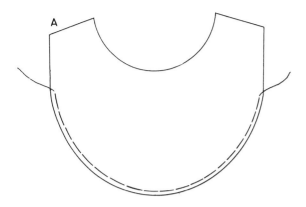

2. Set-in yoke with curves: Make a row of *gathering stitches* 6 mm from the outer curved edge, stitching from the wrong side of the fabric (A). Turn in this edge 15 mm; pin. Pull up gathering-thread until seam allowance will lie flat. Tie ends securely. Distribute fullness evenly. Press edge removing pins as you work (B). Place yoke over garment with raw edges even; pin. From the outside, *edge-stitch* yoke in place (C). Yoke may be top-stitched same as yoke with corners and the facing may be stitched in place same as steps C and D.

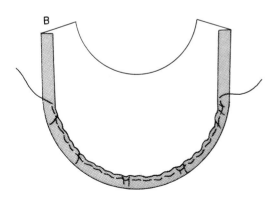

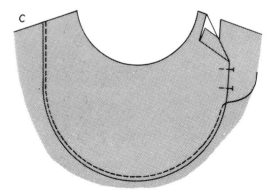

Z

Zipper

A fastener that became popular in the 1940s. It has two strips of fabric with interlocking edges that open and close with a sliding gadget. There's a style of zipper suitable for every garment. Some are inserted to be as unnoticeable as possible while others are meant to show. The invisible zipper is the newest type and each manufacturer gives specific instructions for inserting their own product.

Be sure to match zipper weight to fabric weight. A heavy zipper may pull or distort an opening in a soft lightweight fabric. Stitch zipper to the garment sections before they are joined to other sections, if possible.

Even after the garment has been cut out, it may be possible to eliminate the zipper if the neck opening is large enough to slip over your head easily. Simply stitch the garment and facing seams shut as you work.

The easiest type to insert is the neckline zipper centred under the opening. The exposed zipper methods chosen are quick and easy shortcuts to a unique application.

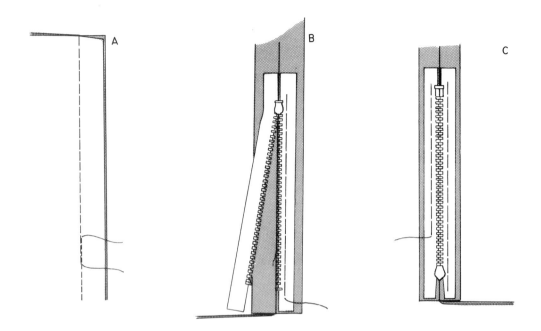

1. Centre application: All you need is a zipper—
no pins. *Stitch* garment sections together to zipper
symbol; *back-stitch* and break stitching. *Machine-
baste* zipper opening along seamline (A). *Press*
entire seam open. With garment upside down,
extend seam allowances next to zipper foot. Open
zipper and place face down on extended seam
allowances, with open end of zipper at edge of
seam and the teeth or coil along the basted seam.
Machine-baste zipper tape to extended seam allowance (B). Folding fabric under the machine
head so it will handle easier; machine-baste
remaining tape to extended seam allowance, starting at the zipper stop (C). Mark end of zipper with
pin on the outside of the seam. Stitch 6 mm from
basted seam through all thicknesses, pivoting at
the corners as you stitch across the end of the
zipper (D).

Note: The remaining zipper application techniques are given for standard size teeth or coils. For
zippers with larger teeth or coils, adjust opening
width so it may be opened and closed easily.

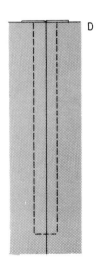

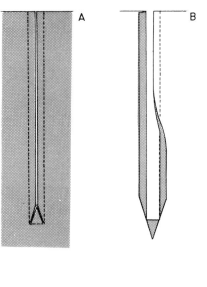

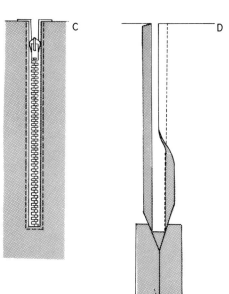

2. Exposed zipper with stitched opening: Use this zipper with or without a seam. Draw a line down the centre of the garment. Lay zipper over line and mark where the stop ends. Using *reinforcement stitches,* stitch 6 mm from each side of the line, *pivoting* at corners opposite the end mark. Slash along line, *clipping* diagonally to corner stitches (A). Turn in raw edges along stitching; *press* (B). Centre zipper under opening edges; pin. *Edge-stitch* garment to zipper tape (C).

To insert in a seam, machine-baste zipper opening shut. Trim seam allowances to 3 mm about 6 mm above end of seam. Stitch same as step A (D) remove basting, then clip diagonally and complete same as steps B and C without a seam.

3. Exposed zipper with faced opening: Cut a 88 mm wide self-fabric strip the length of the zipper tapes plus 38–50 mm. Shape one end as desired. Turn in long raw edges and shaped end 10 mm; press. Draw a line down the centre of the strip and mark where zipper stop ends (A). Centre strip over garment area, placing right side of strip on the wrong side of the garment. *Stitch* 6 mm from each side of line, *pivoting* at corners opposite the end mark. Slash along line, *clipping* diagonally to corner stitches (B). Turn facing to outside along stitches; press. *Edge-stitch* close to outer pressed edge and then stitch again 6 mm away (C). Centre closed zipper under opening edges; pin. Edge-stitch garment to zipper tape and again 6 mm away (D).

4. Exposed decorative zipper: Prepare opening same as method 2, steps A or D above. Turn raw edges to outside along stitching; press. Centre zipper under opening edges; pin. *Edge-stitch* zipper in place (A). Lap trim over raw edges, *mitring* corners at ends of zipper; pin. Edge-stitch both edges of trim in place (B).

To insert a zipper in leathers and fake leathers and furs, see A Fast Start.

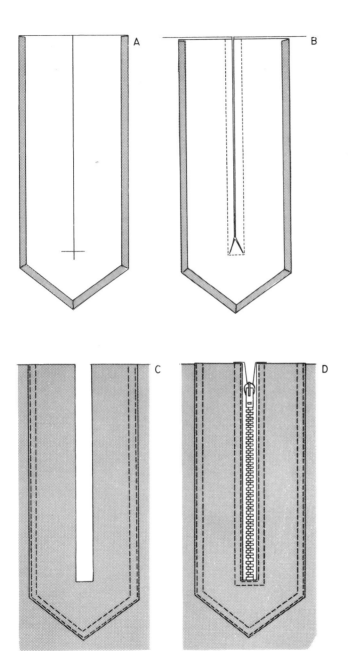

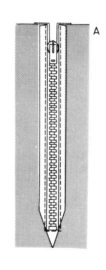

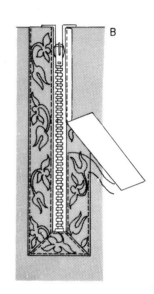